"Jon Friedman understands that the genius of
Bob Dylan (resiliency and reinvention) is also the key
to creating a life of innovation and joy. It is our rebel
artists like Dylan who create the unique cultural
stew that keeps us forever young."

—Jonathan Taplin, director of USC Annenberg
Innovation Lab and author of *Outlaw Blues:
Adventures in the Counter-Culture Wars*

Forget About Today

BOB DYLAN'S GENIUS FOR (RE)INVENTION,
SHUNNING THE NAYSAYERS,
AND CREATING A PERSONAL REVOLUTION

Jon Friedman

A PERIGEE BOOK

A PERIGEE BOOK
Published by the Penguin Group
Penguin Group (USA) Inc.
375 Hudson Street, New York, New York 10014, USA

Penguin Group (Canada), 90 Eglinton Avenue East, Suite 700, Toronto, Ontario M4P
2Y3, Canada (a division of Pearson Penguin Canada Inc.) • Penguin Books Ltd., 80 Strand,
London WC2R 0RL, England • Penguin Group Ireland, 25 St. Stephen's Green, Dublin 2,
Ireland (a division of Penguin Books Ltd.) • Penguin Group (Australia), 250 Camberwell
Road, Camberwell, Victoria 3124, Australia (a division of Pearson Australia Group Pty.
Ltd.) • Penguin Books India Pvt. Ltd., 11 Community Centre, Panchsheel Park, New
Delhi—110 017, India • Penguin Group (NZ), 67 Apollo Drive, Rosedale, Auckland 0632,
New Zealand (a division of Pearson New Zealand Ltd.) • Penguin Books (South Africa)
(Pty.) Ltd., 24 Sturdee Avenue, Rosebank, Johannesburg 2196, South Africa
Penguin Books Ltd., Registered Offices: 80 Strand, London WC2R 0RL, England

While the author has made every effort to provide accurate telephone numbers, Internet
addresses, and other contact information at the time of publication, neither the publisher
nor the author assumes any responsibility for errors, or for changes that occur after
publication. Further, the publisher does not have any control over and does not assume
any responsibility for author or third-party websites or their content.

Copyright © 2012 by Jon Friedman
Text design by Tiffany Estreicher

First edition: August 2012

Library of Congress Cataloging-in-Publication Data

Friedman, Jon, 1955–
Forget about today : Bob Dylan's genius for (re)invention, shunning the naysayers, and
creating a personal revolution / Jon Friedman.—1st ed.
p.   cm.
ISBN 978-0-399-53754-7
1. Dylan, Bob, 1941– 2. Self-help techniques. I. Title.
ML420.D98F75   2012
782.42164092—dc23   2012014180

PRINTED IN THE UNITED STATES OF AMERICA

10 9 8 7 6 5 4 3 2 1

Most Perigee books are available at special quantity discounts for bulk purchases for sales
promotions, premiums, fund-raising, or educational use. Special books, or book excerpts,
can also be created to fit specific needs. For details, write: Special Markets, Penguin Group
(USA) Inc., 375 Hudson Street, New York, New York 10014.

ALWAYS LEARNING   PEARSON

To Mark Friedman, Jordan Karen, Marissa Karen,
and Ali Karen, the best nephews and nieces in the world:
May you stay forever young!

Contents

Introduction

BOB DYLAN, A SELF-HELP GURU?

You bet.

Since Dylan burst onto the music scene in 1961, critics, pundits, and fans alike have celebrated his remarkable skills as a songwriter, poet, vocalist, and performer of folk and rock 'n' roll music. Although I agree with this assessment, I also believe that it doesn't quite do the man justice. He represents so much more to me than an entertainer.

That's why I wanted to write this book. I think Dylan can teach people life lessons based on his mysterious genius. He stands for longevity, the quality that we all hope to achieve in our careers. Can you think of anybody in your field who has thrived for fifty-plus years and still appears to be going strong? Consider that Dylan completed work in March 2012 on his thirty-fifth studio album.

What's most impressive about Dylan's legacy is that he has accomplished everything on his own terms. If anything, Dylan's closely held principles probably held him back at various times, such as when this twenty-one-year-old walked off *The Ed Sullivan Show*, the most popular television program of the day, because the producers wouldn't let him sing the song he had chosen for his big night. Dylan could have benefited enormously from the supersonic push from an appearance on *Ed Sullivan*. But he refused to betray his ideals.

Throughout his five-decade career, he has demonstrated time and again that he will do what he wants, and commercial incentives won't sway him off course. It's not always easy to stick to your beliefs when the promise of something great exists. I don't know how many of us would refuse to make compromises the way Dylan did.

No, we can't learn from Dylan how to write an

anthem like "Blowin' in the Wind" or sing a classic such as "Like a Rolling Stone." My purpose is to go beyond the songs and try to understand how Dylan has been able to remain in our collective consciousness for all of these years.

How long has Dylan been in our lives? Remember, he arrived in Greenwich Village from his native Midwest the same week that John F. Kennedy was sworn in as the nation's thirty-fifth president.

I view Dylan through a prism other than music. I consider his lifetime of success and hold him up as a role model. Indeed, Dylan inspires people. We have seen presidents, corporate titans, movie stars, athletes, and philanthropists embraced as self-help icons because they supply wisdom and give hope to their supporters. They have a great deal to offer. I put Dylan in the company of these other high achievers because we can all learn so much from studying his example of success.

Think about it. Not many people in any field can match his staying power. His ability to endure in the entertainment industry, in particular, for five decades astounds me. Dylan has thrived in the most public of professions. He has not been perfect, God knows. He has made some foolish moves, and sometimes he didn't respond automatically to the changes swirling around him. And by insisting on doing things his way all the time, he has appeared to the public to be stubborn and aloof. But after every disappointment and apparent defeat, Dylan has managed to pull himself up off the canvas.

I can respect his grit and tenacity as much as his proclivity for writing and singing "Blowin' in the Wind," "The Times They Are a-Changin'," "Mr. Tambourine Man," "Like a Rolling Stone," "The Man in Me," "Tangled Up in Blue," "Every Grain of Sand," "Jokerman," "Not Dark Yet," "Things Have Changed," "Mississippi," "Working Man's Blues #2," and so many other gems from his back pages.

I don't intend to write strictly about Dylan's musical triumphs. Studying his life, I see him in a bigger picture. Yes, Dylan possesses special talents. But his natural ability alone is not what has enabled him to remain so relevant and vital for such a long period of time.

What has kept him in the game is his perseverance, his work ethic, his passion for doing the work, his competitiveness, and his ability to convert defeats into victories. These are also the hallmarks of any successful individual in sports or business or politics or the arts. In other words, Dylan can serve somebody as a role model in any walk of life. You don't have to be a musical peer of his—though he has influenced scores of songwriters and singers—to see his value and learn from his example.

I'm not a musician, and Bob Dylan has meant a lot to me over the years. I appreciate his versatility and marvel at his endurance and his sense of vision as a folkie, a pop star, a country crooner, a gospel singer, and a bluesman.

As a journalist who tries to make sense out of the world, I can also recognize a person who has an extraordinary commitment to what he is doing. Dylan is a millionaire many times over, but he isn't all about making money. He is that rarity who lives his life on his own terms, not those of his employers. That kind of success alone is as admirable as any of his musical accomplishments.

Dylan has long demonstrated resilience. He has found the strength of purpose to mount comebacks and prove to skeptics that he can bend with the changing times. He proved his mettle after falling into a steep decline throughout the 1980s. By his own admission in *Chronicles: Volume One*, his engrossing 2004 memoir, Dylan had lost his muse. Further, he seemed to be out of step with the video-crazed music industry and the "Morning in America"–oriented United States.

But tellingly, he set out to show the public that he still belonged. His strategy of nonstop touring around the world, for example, worked brilliantly. His decision to launch what the media came to call the Never Ending Tour confirmed Dylan's innate business acumen, as he methodically tapped a new and fertile market. New fans discovered him and reveled in the same qualities that a previous generation of followers had appreciated.

The idea for this book grew out of a reliable source: Dylan himself. In *Chronicles*, Dylan wrote extensively about what critics and fans have written off as his fallow period, the 1980s. Dylan himself doesn't shy away from the outside criticism and actually proves to be his own harshest critic in the book.

To see Dylan today, it's hard to imagine that he went through a decade-long slump. He is riding high now. His albums sell well, and he has the clout, and the chops, to play about one hundred shows a year around the world. He is beloved by a generation of fans that wasn't even born yet when, in the mid-1970s, he was polishing off *Blood on the Tracks*, often hailed as his best album.

Dylan explained in *Chronicles* that he set out on the Never Ending Tour on a deliberate and thoughtful course of action to regain his relevance in our lives. This idea intrigued me—that this brilliant musician had the wherewithal to craft such an ambitious and ultimately successful strategy for his comeback. It's the kind of case study you might find at a graduate school of business: "Reviving a Damaged Brand and Making It Highly Relevant Once Again."

A few words now about the title of this book: *Forget About Today* is a phrase from Dylan's gem "Mr. Tambourine Man" (which not so coincidentally is my favorite Dylan song). It represents a concept that he has lived, and it stands as the cornerstone of his longevity.

He has proven the value of forging ahead and not letting success or failure overwhelm him. You will read in the ensuing chapters how Dylan has done this.

It's my hope that you will embrace the kinds of life

lessons that Dylan has carried out for himself. It's tricky for me, writing about such a powerful presence—and one who is still intent on breaking new ground at every turn, in music, art, and prose writing.

Sure, critics are bound to carp that Dylan's voice is too raspy and rough these days. Some even suggest that maybe he should leave the road for good.

If he took the time to read such stuff, he'd probably shake his head in bemusement. Maybe he'd laugh at the irony that the naysayers are saying today what short-sighted reviewers were writing fifty years ago: Bob Dylan can't sing. They didn't get it then, and they don't get it now. Dylan lives his life as an artist, not as a crowd pleaser, and yet he is getting the last laugh on all his detractors. Dylan continues to do whatever he wants. That lesson in itself is a pretty powerful one, too.

In case you were wondering, Dylan did not talk with me for this project. When I initially requested time with him, I was asked to submit a formal interview request by email and did so. Through his highly professional and compassionate representative, Dylan politely declined the invitation to talk. I couldn't feel too badly about the rejection. Dylan seldom grants interviews to authors and usually speaks publicly only when it serves his needs, such as upon the release of a new album. This is not exactly shocking. Most entertainment people have the same game plan because they feel they don't need the publicity. Besides, public figures protect their privacy by nature, and they're wary of the motivations of reporters.

Nor did I seek Bob Dylan's approval to write this book. The opinions expressed on these pages are all mine, though I conducted hundreds of interviews with musicians, journalists, corporate executives, and friends who have followed Dylan's utterances for most of their lives.

Primarily, I don't want to present to the world yet another Dylan biography. Likewise, my mission is not to reveal the identity of "Mr. Jones" by offering the millionth speculative theory on the subject. I prefer to keep the parlor games in the parlor.

It was my hope to write something more thoughtful and original here. Dylan has inspired me, and my guess is that he has inspired you as well.

One

KEEP ON
KEEPIN' ON

A hallmark of Bob Dylan's success can be summarized best as "keep on keepin' on." Not only is this one of Dylan's most memorable set of lyrics, from his evocative song "Tangled Up in Blue," but it also underscores a long-held philosophy of his, not to mention an essential reason for his longevity over the past half century.

Throughout his career, Dylan has made action his mantra. He challenges himself to forge ahead, no matter what. In good and bad times, he does what needs to be done. Though this may seem like an obvious point, too many of us fall into the trap of merely *wishing* for something better without actually doing anything about it. It is far easier to talk than to act, which is why most dreams and plans fizzle before they can even begin.

This chapter focuses on an undervalued aspect of Dylan's success, one that anyone can benefit from. You don't have to be necessarily talented or gifted. No special skill is required, either. You don't even have to be 100 percent on the right track all the time. You just have to be *committed* to following through on your plans, getting things done, and moving ahead.

Success Is a Verb

A perfect example of Dylan's commitment was on display on the night of March 25, 2001, when he won the Academy Award for Best Original Song in recognition of his theme to *Wonder Boys*, "Things Have Changed." *Wonder Boys* was a smart film about a middle-aged man chasing the glory of his youthful triumphs. When presenter Jennifer Lopez announced Dylan's name, the hall exploded into a round of loud and sustained applause. The folks watching on television could even hear a fan in the crowd yell out triumphantly, "Whoo!"

Even if Lopez hadn't referred to the winning song as "mirroring the ongoing career of Bob Dylan," the parallels wouldn't have been lost on the Hollywood audience. The entertainment industry's stock-in-trade was just the kind of rise-fall-and-rise-again saga that marked Dylan's annals. As the film's director Curtis Hanson pointed out in one of the bonus features on the *Wonder Boys* DVD, "Who knows more about being a wonder boy and the trap it can be, about the expectations and the fear of repeating yourself?"

Who, indeed? Dylan, who earned acclaim at the precocious age of twenty-one only to fall later into near oblivion, had just proven he was back on top again. It was a wonderfully poignant moment.

As the triumphant Dylan gushed, "Oh, good God— this is amazing!" to the Academy Award show's television audience, he demonstrated the very quality that set him apart from everyone else and enabled him to persevere where others had failed. Of course, a star of his stature could have rearranged his touring schedule to receive his award in person. He could have stayed in Los Angeles and gone to the show-biz parties, where he would have been treated like royalty. But he chose to remain on tour, in Australia, and accept his honor via satellite while standing on, appropriately enough, a concert stage. Keep on keepin' on, indeed.

More than anyone among his peers, Dylan is committed to *doing* what a working musician does. Sure, he enjoys the perks of the job, the recognition, the validation, and the admiration of the fans. But he knows those are sideshows. Accolades, by definition, point to the past. "Nostalgia is death," as Dylan once bluntly put it in an interview with journalist Robert Hilburn of the *Los Angeles Times* at around the time he turned fifty years old.

Yes, we all need a pat on the back now and then. But nobody should confuse a sense of past accomplishment with actual new accomplishment. To move forward, Dylan knew he couldn't simply coast on the static coattails of the past. As Dylan pointed out in his memoir, "It's nice to be known as a legend, and people will pay to see one, but for most people, once is enough." He knows that continued success comes from challenging yourself day in and day out, again and again.

Greatness Through Repetition

Dylan, for all of his superstardom, doesn't shy away from the nitty-gritty of what a devoted musician does—that is, composing, rehearsing, touring, and performing in concert halls around the world.

How, we ask, can the man draw a sense of satisfaction from playing a hundred shows a year around the world without feeling as though it is all an utter grind, what with the constant traveling, rehearsing, and rigors of performing every night? And how the heck can he perform "Like a Rolling Stone" or "All Along the Watchtower" at virtually every gig without feeling bored by the sheer repetition of the task?

Seeking an answer to these mysteries, I asked no less of a Bob Dylan authority than Robbie Robertson. The leader of the Band and a brilliant songwriter in his own right, Robertson started playing lead guitar with Dylan in 1965 and continued to be his bandleader for much of the time through 1974. He had a succinct and indisputable answer.

"It's the thrill of discovery that keeps Bob going," Robertson said.

Rather than regarding repetition as drudgery, Dylan revels in putting himself out there and honing his craft. Sometimes he's on fire; sometimes he seems lackadaisical. That's not the point. Night after night, he's proving himself all over again, rediscovering the beauty and power of his songs as well as the value of his craft. And so are his audiences. He has created a whole new art form out of performing.

Dylan's ability to focus on the controllable aspects of the moment is a critical trait. The process of trial and error can yield unexpected breakthroughs and inspiration that comes only from persistent action.

Dylan personified this point in the early 1990s, after the release of the poorly received album *Under the Red Sky*. Weary and out of inspiration, he challenged himself to stay productive even if it meant recording songs in the privacy of his garage, not some glamorous recording studio, complete with his dog barking in the background. (That scenario actually occurred when he recorded a demo of what would quickly be regarded as one of his most iconic songs, "Every Grain of Sand.")

Alone in his home studio, he tinkered without feeling the pressure of having to produce a blockbuster album. Dylan started recording some of the old folk songs. Once, he had played the tunes as an upstart teenager in Greenwich Village. Three decades later, the material had greater meaning for him, now that he was armed with the wisdom of a fifty-something-year-old man. The result was two modest but important albums: *Good As I Been to You* and *World Gone Wrong*. Though neither would prove to be big commercial hits, the two works inspired Dylan to eventually write the songs that would wind up on his next album, 1997's Grammy-winning *Time Out of Mind*. That was a special achievement in its own right, but I would argue that it would not have been possible without his tinkering on the earlier two albums. Dylan rediscovered his muse, his voice, and his sense of purpose. Some would insist that he had taken a step back by retreating to his garage, but the larger point is that he kept working all the time.

Anyone looking for breakthroughs, whether it's in sports, a new career, or any long-held dream, could learn from Dylan's approach. He went back to the basics and found inspiration. This approach contains a universal application, too. Salespeople, for instance, know this lesson well. At some point, it's a numbers game. You have to knock on so many doors to be successful.

Next time you feel in a rut or discouraged by lack of progress toward a goal, pay attention to the amount of effort you are putting into it. For example, say you're doing fifty sit-ups without the result you want; it may just mean you need to do seventy-five or a hundred. When you come to this realization, you can steel yourself and say, "I can do this." I submit that what we see on the outside as good fortune or extraordinary talent is, more likely than not, the result of persistent action in disguise.

Once, when a journalist asked Dylan to discuss his philosophy for his career, he responded by asking the reporter if he could tell him what a bricklayer's philosophy was. The reporter probably went back to the newsroom and told his editor that Dylan had been putting him on, as he is puckishly wont to do with the media. But Dylan's reply makes perfect sense when you tie it into his value system. The man sees himself as a craftsman, who knows that true mastery of his craft can come only from doing something again and again.

You Don't Rob the Same Bank Twice

Don't confuse genuine productivity for mindless action. Doing the same thing and expecting a different result, as the saying goes, is the definition of insanity. This is not what Dylan advocates for himself.

Everything he does is infused with a sense of intention and innovation. In the late-1980s, for example, after countless tours of the biggest arenas, Dylan told his management he was shaking things up. Dylan said he was going to visit places where he'd never played. He wanted to go to small halls and college campuses—and by the way, he was going to visit those same places again and again, year after year.

Naturally, his skeptical team objected. After all, the conventional wisdom of show business ordained that this was not what a big-time star was supposed to do. Elliot Roberts, who was arranging Dylan's tours at the time, told the star, "You're Jesse James. You don't rob the same bank twice."

Dylan knew instinctively that Roberts was wrong. He knew better because he was the guy who went up on stage and put himself on the line. He, not his advisors watching from the wings, could see the looks on the faces of the audience members. Dylan knew when he was moving them—and, more importantly, when he wasn't turning them on.

How long, he began to fret, could he get the same fans to pay top dollar to see him play the same hits in soulless hockey arenas? Dylan knew that by playing smaller venues in the same cities time after time, and by pricing those tickets more reasonably, the coveted young fans would get used to returning to see him perform.

No, these would not be the kind of big-payday shows that his peers were getting rich from. Dylan sensed, though, that those kinds of audiences were already dwindling. He knew he needed to do it differently even if none of the so-called experts thought so.

Successful people believe in themselves. They trust their instincts; they know that they can do it. Half the battle is in our minds. If we are determined and believe we can succeed, we are more than halfway to achieving our goal.

The opposite of confidence is fear and self-doubt. We are afraid of failure, but fear mostly exists in our minds. Instead of becoming overwhelmed with fear, why not focus on attaining success instead?

Dylan's fans didn't always know what they wanted from him, but the man himself possessed the confidence to know what *he* wanted. He could not have known the outcome, but he had the faith to bet on himself and his instincts. He set out to build a new base by doing what he knew how to do best: perform.

In this case, he was right on the mark. Because he covers so much territory, both geographically and musically, audiences have gotten to know his songs, embracing the live performances as well as the studio recordings of his entire catalog. He has attracted legions of new fans as a result.

How do you know if you're on the right track? You don't. You can't always know. But the trick is to push yourself. You can always do more and do it better. Little by little, your confidence will build, but it can only grow through the act of doing.

A Series of Small Steps

If you are working toward a big goal or dream, the task can seem insurmountable. You may not know where to start, and in view of the mountain of tasks ahead, it's tempting to procrastinate or simply give up before you really get started.

In this respect, we are all the same. And yet, if you

wonder how people achieve big things—where they find the energy, time, and stamina for it—the answer is often simple. They just do it.

The trick is to take one step at a time. Remember, if you don't start, it will never happen at all. What is the very first baby step in the direction of your goal? Just focus on your first step, and when that one is done, focus on the next one, but only that one; don't look too far ahead and get disheartened or overwhelmed. You just need to take the plunge.

Action has always been a hallmark of Dylan's career. At the age of nineteen, he dropped out of the University of Minnesota midway through his sophomore year and moved to Greenwich Village in January 1961 in his quest to make his mark as a folksinger.

"Going to New York was like going to the moon," Dylan told Cameron Crowe in one of his most comprehensive and revealing interviews ever, published as part of the retrospective musical collection *Biograph* in 1985. "You just didn't get on a plane and go there, you know. New York! Ed Sullivan, the New York Yankees, Broadway, Harlem . . . you might as well have been talking about China. It was some place where not many people had ever gone, and anybody who did go never came back."

Dylan's decision to drop out of school took a lot of guts. As an undergraduate at the largest university in his home state, Dylan had all the security that a Minnesota teenager could have hoped for in President Dwight Eisenhower's America. But by then Dylan had clearly developed the self-reliance required for such a life-altering gambit. He knew he had to take a bold step. He was gambling on his ability and determination—and, in the parlance of Las Vegas, he was all in.

Doing Begets Opportunity

The smallest of actions, even the ones that seem trivial and insignificant, can lead to success. Sometimes opportunity presents itself only while you are in the act of doing something else. Action begets opportunity.

An apt illustration of this point occurred in July 1975,

when Dylan was getting the itch to record an album of new songs. Time was on his side. The clock wasn't ticking. He no longer felt the burden of constantly coming up with new material to satisfy the demands of his record label. "That pressure is off," Dylan told radio interviewer Mary Travers in March 1975. His highly successful album *Blood on the Tracks* had just come out, and it had been received extremely well by critics and fans alike. The challenge, then, was more personal for Dylan. How could the man follow it up? Eager not to repeat himself, he determined that he needed to come up with a new kind of sound, something his audience would never expect.

With this goal in mind, he was driving in Manhattan one afternoon when he spotted a striking-looking woman walking on the sidewalk. She stood out for two reasons. She had very long black hair and was carrying a violin case. Voilà! He pulled over to the curb and struck up a friendly conversation with the musician, whom he had never before met.

Acting on a creative impulse, he invited this total stranger to accompany him to a nearby recording studio.

She agreed and so impressed Dylan with her creative style of playing that he promptly asked her to join his band. The musician turned out to be Scarlet Rivera, and her forceful violin sound became an important component on Dylan's next album, the highly successful *Desire*.

Let's face it. Most of us would have probably kept right on driving and, afraid of leaving our comfort zone or embarrassing ourselves, never dared to take such a chance. But Dylan, showing his innate knack for making his own breaks, took a shot by creating a whole new sound for himself, and it worked out rather well. *Desire* would prove to be the ideal follow-up to *Blood on the Tracks*, yet another triumph of innovation for the ever-restless and ambitious Bob Dylan.

When you focus too much on getting *there* instead of *here*, you lose the energy and passion that dwells in that moment. Yes, it takes discipline to embrace the present, but remember, the *journey* itself is the main event. When you start on a course of action, you put yourself on a road filled with surprises. If you forge ahead with only the end result in mind, you can miss important signals along the way. But if you are open and ready to act, who knows what can happen?

The Philosophy of Keep on Keepin' On

It's easy to dream and imagine a better life, but you also need to give form to your thoughts with decisive action. And that's where most of us get stuck. To create positive change, you need to take positive action.

Too many people stop short of action. We know this is a common pitfall of businesses in which the focus is on strategy and planning and not so much on execution. The same phenomenon happens to individuals. How many days and nights do you spend dreaming about what could be? Now think about it: What if you devoted the same amount of time to doing things to make it a reality? What would happen?

Without action, you could have the greatest idea and

the greatest plan in the world and you would still fail. On the other hand, a modest idea coupled with a still-incomplete plan can often produce success when accompanied by enough action.

The best part of this lesson is that anyone can apply it—this is not some innate gift. If you can see the goal and if you have an idea of where you're going as well as some semblance of how you're going to get there, then you are already ahead of most people.

Two

THE FINE ART
OF PISSING
PEOPLE OFF

B ob Dylan has gained so much from pissing people off that he has practically made an art form out of the practice. He deliberately invents scenarios in which he can assert himself as a provocateur. This stands out as one of the traits that separate him from the rest of us. Most of us tend to shy away from confrontations. They make us feel uncomfortable. Not Dylan. He understands the benefits of pushing people's buttons. Ultimately, his ability to piss people off has played a large part in his longevity and knack for reinventing himself.

From his days as an up-and-coming folksinger in

Greenwich Village in the early 1960s to his controversial performances in China in April 2011, Dylan has willfully irritated, enraged, and infuriated fans and critics alike. But these acts are not at all the frivolous pursuits of a mischievous mind. The act of getting people worked up is, in fact, a cornerstone of Dylan's strategic vision for himself as an ever-evolving musician and artist. By doing this, Dylan can succeed in keeping the outsiders off-balance. So, as he immediately creates space for himself, he allows his art to grow. Dylan gains the freedom from the naysayers that he needs so much. He can innovate, experiment, and finally move forward.

Too many of us shy away from rocking the boat. The need to please and get along with people can prevent us from moving forward. But if you don't stand up for yourself, who will? Dylan shows us how crucial it is to assert your value even if it means making people uncomfortable. This is true in good times, naturally, because you want to keep your personal momentum going. But it is absolutely essential for you to do when you don't necessarily hold the upper hand or when you know you'll be upsetting people. We can see that Dylan carried out this valuable lesson going back to the beginning of his career.

Standing Up to the Suits

To his credit, Dylan was pissing people off long before he became a worldwide star. It takes a lot of guts, or some good old-fashioned chutzpah, to put yourself on the line when you have everything to gain simply by keeping quiet and going along with the program. But you have to innately recognize, too, that the rewards are immeasurable in terms of gaining self-confidence and showing people that you mean business. The most instructive example of the young Dylan provoking people occurred when *The Ed Sullivan Show*, then America's number one television variety program, invited him to appear on May 12, 1963. An appearance on this CBS Sunday night institution had helped catapult Dylan's hero Elvis Presley to superstardom in the 1950s, and the fast-talking impresario would repeat the feat when he introduced the Beatles to America in February 1964. Understandably, Dylan, still a few weeks shy of his twenty-second birthday, was thrilled to be asked to perform. He told *Rolling Stone* in 2009 that it was "a dream come true just to be on that stage."

But on the day of the show, a CBS censor overruled Ed Sullivan himself and refused to allow Dylan to come on the show and sing his original composition "Talkin' John Birch Paranoid Blues," a song that lampoons the paranoia about the Communist threat in America during the cold war.

Of course, Dylan could have done what most people in his situation would have decided to do: swallowed his pride, taken the easy way out, and agreed to sing a different song. For instance, "Blowin' in the Wind" would have been an obvious substitution and a wholly acceptable one, at that. Dylan had written the song, and it was about to gain traction as an anthem of the civil rights movement. When Peter, Paul, and Mary later covered it, their radio-friendly version achieved such enormous success that it became the fastest-selling single in the history of Warner Bros. Records. Clearly, with so much riding on this appearance; it made no sense at all for such a young and powerless kid to risk alienating one of the most powerful men in all of television. The smart career move would have been for Dylan to play it safe and sing any damned song that would have kept him on the show. Or would it have?

Even though Dylan needed Sullivan more than Sullivan needed him, he flatly refused to play a more palatable number and promptly bolted from the television studio. "I just had it in my mind to sing that particular song," Dylan told the noted historian Douglas Brinkley, who wrote the *Rolling Stone* cover story in 2009.

As it turned out, Dylan's decision to push back at Ed Sullivan was an inspired act. Dylan transformed his image overnight, from ragamuffin Everyman folksinger to the oppressed victim of CBS's bullyboy corporate censorship. Not only did Dylan attract immediate, favorable write-ups in the press; crucially, this ballsy decision also did wonders to popularize his long-lasting image as a singer and a songwriter of great integrity, a man who represented the underdog in society. Not surprisingly, Dylan soon went on to write such antiestablishment anthems as "The Times They Are a-Changin'." Meanwhile, Dylan's credibility as a principled folksinger soon spread like wildfire. Before long he was invited to sing at the historic civil rights rally in Washington, DC, on August 28, 1963, on the afternoon when the Reverend Martin Luther King Jr. delivered his stirring "I Have a Dream" speech. Pundits began to refer to Dylan as the spokesman for his generation. No wonder Brinkley noted in his *Rolling Stone* piece: "Bolting from *The Ed Sullivan Show* was the true turning point in Dylan's life script."

More than any of his counterparts in popular music, Dylan is revered because he lives his principles. This is why he can sound totally credible when he sings such moving songs decrying injustice as "The Lonesome Death of Hattie Carroll," "Percy's Song," "Hurricane," and "Lenny Bruce." It's also why John Lennon, Paul McCartney, George Harrison, Paul Simon, Phil Ochs, Tracy Chapman, Neil Young, Bruce Springsteen, Bono, Sinéad O'Connor, and many other songwriters have so admired Dylan through the years. They see that Dylan isn't afraid to challenge people and even anger them.

In 1963, Bob Dylan needed Ed Sullivan more than Sullivan needed Dylan, but by not being afraid to assert himself, Dylan came out ahead. How many of us would have stood up to the powers-that-be and lost the chance of a lifetime? I bet you, not many. But in every situation, you have to ask yourself, Am I just going along because I'm afraid to rock the boat? If you truly believe in something, however small, it's worth standing up for.

That was the point in his life when Dylan drew a line in the sand and showed himself and the rest of the world that he would be willing to sacrifice a quick fix—a national TV appearance!—for his principles. And he didn't do it quietly; he told the biggest name in TV entertainment that he would not play ball. The decision changed the path of his career.

Five decades later, Dylan is still calling the shots and doesn't get overly impressed by any suit, even when it is being worn by the leader of the free world. Just see what President Barack Obama told *Rolling Stone* in 2010:

Here's what I love about Dylan: He was exactly as you'd expect he would be. He wouldn't come to the rehearsal; usually, all these guys are practicing before the set in the evening. He didn't want to take a picture with me; usually all the talent is dying to take a picture with me and Michelle before the show, but he didn't show up to that. He came in and played "The Times They Are a-Changin'." A beautiful rendition. The guy is so steeped in this stuff that he can just come up with some new arrangement, and the song sounds completely different. Finishes the song, steps off the stage . . . comes up, shakes my hand, sort of tips his head, gives me just a little grin, and then leaves. . . . That was our only interaction with him. And I thought: That's how you want Bob Dylan, right? You don't want him to be all cheesin' and grinnin' with you. You want him to be a little skeptical about the whole enterprise.

Electric Shock

Undoubtedly, the most infamous example of Dylan pissing people off occurred on July 25, 1965. On that fateful

Sunday night, Dylan took the stage at the annual Newport Folk Festival to resounding cheers, befitting his status as the king of folk music and in tribute to his triumphs there in 1963 and 1964. But as soon as he and the raucous Butterfield Blues Band plugged in, the crowd gasped. "They certainly booed, I'll tell you that—you could hear it all over the place," Dylan recalled five months later during a televised press conference in San Francisco. In the annals of musical performance, the only precedent took place in May 1913, when Igor Stravinsky debuted his ballet *The Rite of Spring* and sparked a riot. But Dylan knew exactly what he was doing on that tumultuous summer night in Rhode Island.

What Dylan neglected to say at the press conference was the most telling point of all: He intended to shock people when he went electric. He sought to unsettle them. Though it seemed he was determined to throw dirt on the grave of his folk legacy in the most public and provocative way possible, and at all costs, Dylan had a strategic objective.

Dylan had outpaced his contemporaries in the folk community. By 1963, the folk breakout *The Freewheelin'*

Bob Dylan was his ticket to the big time. It was his first big-selling album and the first one that caught the attention of people outside the close-knit folk world. Everyone in Greenwich Village had cheered his success because it lifted the entire genre. His impact was so significant he might have rested on those laurels for the rest of his career. Pete Seeger had. Dave Van Ronk had. Phil Ochs had. Even Joan Baez had. Any one of them would have told Dylan this was no time to change course. These were his friends, his colleagues, people who boosted his career. And he was about to be accused of betraying them all.

"I was doing fine the way I was going," Dylan told interviewers about this period. But if he had played it safe, continuing to churn out folk hits, he surely would have become a period curio. Like such immensely talented peers as Seeger, Van Ronk, Ochs, and Baez, he would have been identified with folk music forever. Dylan wanted more out of his work.

Dylan saw the handwriting on the wall. He'd heard the Beatles' "I Want to Hold Your Hand" (famously mistaking the line "I can't hide" for the more risqué "I get high") and the Animals' brilliant cover of "The House of the Rising Sun," a Dylan folk staple, and he knew that the future was now; he would have to reinvent himself. To do that, he would need to turn his back on the thing that made him what he was. He became aware of the power of the Beatles while driving cross-country that February. He marveled out in Colorado that the British quartet had amassed eight songs in the charts. Eight songs! The times were definitely changing.

By going electric, Dylan dared to do something that most of us wouldn't have the courage to do in our own lives: tamper with our track record of success. We study hard in school, start at the bottom of a company, work overtime slavishly, take constant guff from bosses, and claw our way up the corporate ladder—all in the hope of making a name for ourselves in our field. The last thing any of us would deliberately do at that point is to undermine our hard-won achievements. But at some point, success is a trap. You can start to coast and slide. It's a slippery slope, devoting all of your time toward holding on to what you have, rather than pondering new ways to innovate and build something different.

When you find yourself losing ground, Dylan's way may be the only route back up again. You have to expect—no, welcome—resistance. Like Dylan, you must revel in your ability to challenge people's impressions of you. And if you happen to cause a commotion along the way, so be it. Just before he took the stage for his first post-Newport concert, a month later at the West Side Tennis Club at Forest Hills in New York City, Dylan gathered his musicians in a football-style huddle backstage and excitedly told them: "It's gonna be a circus out there!"

You must be willing to put yourself in the middle of the circus if you're going to make change in your life. Dylan was 100 percent willing to provoke people, and you should be, too, if it serves your objective. Robbie Robertson played lead guitar during Dylan's electric concerts in 1965 and 1966, and he recognized Dylan's extraordinary belief in his choice. "He believed so much in what he was doing. Nothing was going to stop him."

So it was in July 1965 that a crowd of more than a hundred thousand flocked to Newport to see Dylan perform his folk hits as the solo-acoustic troubadour they had come to know and love and nearly deify. There was a long delay before he came on, and the crowd grew restless. When Dylan walked onstage that night, wearing a leather jacket and an electric Fender Stratocaster guitar, spectators, already antsy, knew something was different. He got only as far as a few bars of "Maggie's Farm" when the booing started. The pressure intensified as he launched into the third song, "Like a Rolling Stone," the first time the song had been played in front of a live audience. Pete Seeger supposedly grabbed an ax and headed for the soundboard, to cut the cables to the speakers rather than listen to the abomination before him.

Dylan was visibly shaken but knew in his heart that if he gave them what they wanted, there would be nothing left for him. He'd end up heading for Las Vegas and playing the same greatest hits for the next twenty-five years. Dylan's under-rehearsed band barely played for twenty minutes, but they changed the course of Dylan's career forever.

Tangled Up in Pink

Think of how something as minor and mundane as someone growing a beard or getting a tattoo can automatically become the talk of the office for days. So, imagine the shock that couch potatoes watching *American Idol* got in April 2004 during a commercial for the Victoria's Secret Angels line. It wasn't the supermodel slithering her way through a palazzo in Venice wearing heels, lingerie, and a pair of oversize, feathery wings that made them do a double take. No, it was the appearance of a scruffy, mustachioed, and dare I say devilishly charismatic sixty-something Bob Dylan, accompanied by the song "Love Sick" from his *Time Out of Mind* album.

No sooner did the spot air than accusations flew fast and furious that Dylan had sold out. Again. Throughout his career, Dylan has been accused of being crass and self-serving, but this seemed to take the cake.

Predictably, the nation's headline writers had a field day, too, mocking America's favorite new geriatric sex symbol:

———————

"Bob Dylan Sells Out"
"Bob Dylan Gets Tangled Up in Pink"
"Tangled Up in Boobs"

"We'd considered the headline, 'Dylan Has Gone Positively Madison Avenue,' but it didn't fit our space limitations," Brian Steinberg, then the advertising-beat reporter for the *Wall Street Journal*, told me. "We were shocked—the counterculture was supposed to be free of commercial interests, right? What was going to come next? 'For What It's Worth' in a Coke commercial?"

The reaction of Dylan's fans was positively melodramatic. "I'm going to have to go blow my brains out," wailed John Baky, the curator of Dylan material at La Salle University in Philadelphia, to Steinberg.

But those who accused him of being a shill who would do anything for a big check missed the point entirely. Dylan's motivations have always been more strategic than purely financial, and this case was no different.

Besides, let's face it: Like it or not, it was hardly revolutionary for aging pop stars to align with Madison Avenue. Sting hawked Jaguars, and James Taylor and Michael

---

McDonald gave MCI a hand. In fact, a few years earlier, Dylan himself had allowed the Bank of Montreal to use "The Times They Are a-Changin'" in a television commercial.

But this *was* the same man who had once spat out the lyrics, "Money doesn't talk, it swears." What did it mean when the voice of a generation had become the symbol of capitalism that they had once fought against? Was Dylan selling out?

Yes and no.

To the discerning eye, there was surely a method to Dylan's machinations. Once again, he was showing the world that his image was his—not theirs—to define. He didn't even acknowledge what the naysayers said about him. In fact, he didn't mind at all.

The *Wall Street Journal*'s Steinberg was savvy enough to recognize that there was something happening here, and what it was, was exactly clear.

"He was cognizant of the fact that when Victoria's Secret approached him, it would be a good way to reach a younger audience," Steinberg said. "Radio was not the way to do it anymore, and he had to take matters into his own hands with an innovative way to present his music to a younger audience while keeping his base. Victoria's Secret was upscale, female-focused and it had a reputation for doing beautiful commercials."

At a time when artists of his generation were having a hard time getting mass exposure for their music, Victoria's Secret agreed to feature his CDs for sale in its nationwide retail stores. Dylan would get an opportunity to reach out to young women consumers, a lucrative demographic that went beyond his traditional male base. And the controversy didn't hurt, either, as people of all generations debated his relevance. Dylan, just shy of his sixty-third birthday, proved his ability as a provocateur. Again.

Prepare for Ridicule, Humiliation, and Loneliness

Every time you choose to make a radical, public change in your life, no matter who you may be, you're bound to face not only anger but also something far worse—ridicule.

Most people *dread* the prospect of public criticism and humiliation. We would do anything—*anything*—to avoid being laughed at. So, we play it safe. We don't stick our necks out as far as we should. We censor ourselves and hold back our true spirit, because when we willfully do something passionately, the chances are that somebody will put it down and try hard to crush our spirit.

Do you know what the man who has been lampooned by *Saturday Night Live* many times would say? Bring it on.

He might also add: If they're going to get worked up anyway, why not give them something to really get mad at?

According to Dylan, it's far better to be controversial than irrelevant. How many of us strive to *avoid* controversy? How many times have we aimed to please and make the peace only to lose sight of our goals in the process?

Dylan's former assistant Arthur Rosato has seen many of Dylan's ups and downs and always marvels at his old boss's resolve. Like other people close to Dylan, Rosato drew strength from the man's determination. "I learned so much from him about dealing with criticism," Rosato told me during a phone conversation in 2011. "He knows you're not doing it for them—you're doing it for yourself."

The act of going electric was the turning point for Dylan. What is yours? It takes incredible courage to make a decision that you know will change everything; nevertheless, you have to decide where you want to go, test the waters, and dive in. Sure, the results may not always be spectacular. Dylan certainly encountered disappointment, disillusionment, and setbacks. A year after Newport, a concertgoer called him "Judas" at England's Manchester Free Trade Hall for betraying the folk music tradition. That must have been a blow, but Dylan always managed to lift himself off the canvas and come back a little more resolute and a lot stronger.

You must inoculate yourself against other people's negative reactions and have enough faith in yourself to see things through. As you face the inevitable criticism, how do you find the inner strength to hold your ground?

If you're anything like Dylan, you trust your instincts to know that you are doing what is right for yourself, even though everyone is swearing that it is so very wrong. How many of us would call it quits before even starting? Not Dylan, and that has made all the difference.

Three

FIND FULFILLMENT OUTSIDE OF YOUR COMFORT ZONE

B ob Dylan has built a long record of achievement by stepping out of his comfort zone. Throughout his career, Dylan has rebelled against the concept of security. He has never stayed in the same place for too long. What you or I might see as representing a security blanket in our lives, he regards as stifling. And he felt this way even before he became a star. It has been a lifelong trait. Whether he was at the point of starting out or enjoying a creative peak or trying to make a comeback, he has always pushed himself out of his safety zone.

Dylan has plenty to teach us about flourishing amid

change in our lives. While many of us naturally seek stability, Dylan is at his most innovative and commanding when he has tested himself by jumping into an alien situation. He told then-journalist Nora Ephron in 1965: "I accept chaos." Actually, Dylan *luxuriates* in upheaval. There he finds the freedom to improvise and excel under pressure. He loves in turn to push people out of their comfort zones, in big and small ways. Just ask anyone who's attended one of his concerts during which he suddenly changed a familiar song's tempo or arrangement or invented a set of lyrics that the audience hadn't heard before. He is usually at the top of his game when he doesn't play it safe.

Dylan might have excelled as a corporate strategic planner. He possesses an uncanny ability to identify a deficiency and then act conclusively to convert it into an asset. He applies his intellect to craft a plan and solve whatever roadblock has cropped up. By following his thought process, we can see how his problem-solving mind operates. He has often filled in the blanks in his life by making one decisive move after another. To those of us standing on the outside looking in, it would seem chaotic and even mind-boggling to drop out of college, pull up stakes from where you've experienced profound personal growth, and move across the country to pursue a career in an alien, cutthroat environment. Dylan has made all of these moves.

He's Leaving Home

You could say that the first time Dylan moved out of his comfort zone, he wasn't quite yet "Bob Dylan." He was still known to many as Bobby Zimmerman—remember, his birth name was Robert Allen Zimmerman—when he quit the University of Minnesota during his sophomore year, at the end of 1960. The regimented academic life on a college campus offered him nothing because it couldn't teach him how to do what he'd decided would be his life's work—namely making his mark as a folksinger. In fact, his later memory of college reinforced his earlier presumption that he had been wasting his time inside the classroom. "Colleges are like old-age homes, except for the fact that more people die in colleges than in old-age homes," Dylan told journalist Nat Hentoff in a *Playboy* interview in March 1966. He yearned to get out on the road and finally headed east to New York City, making brief stops at the University of Wisconsin in Madison and in Chicago. How fulfilled Dylan must have felt as he grew ever closer to reaching his objective of seeing the bright lights of the big city! "I'd spent so much time thinking about it," he recollected in an interview with Cameron Crowe in 1985. "I couldn't think about it anymore."

The journey and the new life that awaited Dylan started the moment he made up his mind to move to New York. All these years later, the decision still seems audacious. He was truly going for broke. Remember, Dylan had no safety net whatsoever in the city. In fact, he was nothing more than a blip on New York's landscape. On his first night in town, he performed at a dingy club and had to ask from the stage, where he was playing a set for free, if anyone in the audience knew a place where he might crash for the night. God knows he didn't have a steady job lined up, either. He had to beseech club owners to let him sing on hootenanny nights in the unglamorous basket houses—so named because the entertainers literally passed a basket to the audience (as it were). They hoped that the spectators would kindly give them tips. When Dylan arrived in New York, it's fair to say that all he had was his conviction that he could make it there. He had to; there was no turning back.

When Dylan dropped out of college, it wasn't an idle joyride to get out of going to a biology class or undertake a hippie mission to find himself. Dylan instead had a well-thought-out plan to make it as a folk musician. He reminds us vividly that it's one thing, however daring in theory, to take yourself out of a safe environment, but quite another to follow it up by executing a feasible game plan. Dylan had a strategy, all right. His first objective was to meet his idol Woody Guthrie, the revered songwriter who had written "This Land Is Your Land" and many other Americana classics, and see what a hero looked like up close. It didn't deter Dylan that Guthrie suffered from Huntington's disease, a degenerative illness that severely weakens an individual's muscle coordination, and had great trouble speaking and writing. Dylan visited him many times at a hospital in New Jersey, and a friendship developed, even though Guthrie was incapacitated and twenty-nine years Dylan's senior. By displaying considerable charm, boundless youthful exuberance, and sheer persistence, Dylan won over Guthrie and parlayed his visits into something even more concrete. He inveigled his way into the epicenter of the folk scene. He met such helpful folks as the master of ceremonies at Gerde's Folk City—the most well-regarded folk club in Greenwich Village, where Dylan would eventually make his mark.

Dylan shows us that by exiting your comfort zone, you immediately create an atmosphere for yourself in which to flourish on your terms. It can trigger continuous discoveries, not to mention self-discoveries. Riding the crest of his excitement gave him the impetus to overcome the twin obstacles of not having any professional connections in his new surroundings and not having a track record of accomplishments to fall back on. By challenging himself so severely, he felt alive. Free! The minute he jumped out of the car that had transported him from the Midwest, he recognized that he had just raised the stakes immeasurably in his life. He had pledged to everyone back home that he would move to New York—and, doggone it, he had done just that. Dylan, all of nineteen, thrust himself smack into a do-or-die situation. He would test himself and find out whether he had what it took to make his mark far away from home. The change of scenery made him feel uninhibited and bold. It gave Dylan courage. He was calling the shots. He was about to find out what he was made of.

Within a few months of his breakthrough, Dylan had entrenched himself in the most influential folk music scene in the United States. Once, he could have only dreamed of entering this world. By daring to make his dream come true, Dylan set in motion the start of his career—and the rest of his life. Everything that followed in music and love stemmed from this one act.

Had Dylan remained in Minnesota, he would have probably drifted into obscurity or found limited fulfillment as some sort of regional attraction by performing at state fairs and night after night in local bars. Dylan teaches us a valuable lesson. He knew that the only way he could test himself was to transport himself out of the Twin Cities and relocate to the capital of the folk music scene. "When I arrived in Minneapolis, it had seemed like a big city or a big town. When I left, it was like some rural outpost that you see once from a passing train," Dylan commented in 1985. It's interesting. Dylan was so unheralded in Minneapolis that he was consigned to playing at a pizzeria near the University of Minnesota campus called, of all things, the Purple Onion. When he left for New York City, he was hardly moving from a position of strength. Likely, few in Minneapolis even noticed that he had left. Nor did he miss them much. He didn't have the time, anyway; he was too busy getting on with his life.

Would-be stars imagine descending on New York and taking the town by storm. But they idly think of what might go wrong. They get intimidated by pondering the long odds and decide it makes more sense to play it safe. They go on to attend college or graduate school or they keep their day jobs. They give up on their dreams before they even get started and never give themselves a shot at achieving the success that they've dreamed of attaining. Dylan showed that by lifting yourself out of cozy surroundings, you can bring the best out in yourself. You exceed your expectations. Dylan went from being a face in the crowd in the Twin Cities to becoming the biggest star in Greenwich Village, all in the span of only a year. To make it happen, he had to take himself out of a safe environment and hurtle headfirst into the unknown.

Into the Wilderness

Dylan constantly seeks adventures and challenges because he never feels content to rest on his laurels. He takes absolutely nothing for granted and understands that the future is promised to no one. He has shown an inclination to shake things up even when—especially when—he appears to be standing at the zenith of his popularity and creativity. It's as if his own BS-meter reminds him that he can't afford to sit still just because of what he accomplished yesterday. If he stopped extending himself, he might get complacent and begin to slip. Only by making continual changes in the way he approaches his life and work can Dylan feel certain that he'll keep his creative impulses flowing.

One of the prime examples of Dylan lifting himself out of a safe place for the unknown occurred in February 1966. Less than a year before, Dylan had released his rock masterpiece and first hit single, "Like a Rolling Stone." Yet he then did something revolutionary by the parameters of the music world. The voice of the counterculture, the spokesman of his generation, and the poet laureate of the civil rights movement entered a recording studio in the alien territory of Nashville, Tennessee. This was the acknowledged country music capital of the United States, the home of the Grand Ole Opry and the stomping grounds of the likes of Ernest Tubb and Minnie Pearl, where Dylan set out to record his next rock 'n' roll album, following the landmark success of *Highway 61 Revisited* in 1965. Talk about worlds colliding!

Dylan innately understood that he needed to find a source of fresh inspiration. He didn't want to run the risk of getting stale in New York City. "Like a Rolling Stone" was both a blessing, because its popularity enabled Dylan to break through in rock 'n' roll, and a potential curse, because now everyone wanted Dylan to duplicate that sound so that the label could repeat the hit single's commercial prowess. He had a lot to live up to. And he wanted to show everyone—the suits, the Beatles, not to mention himself—that he was up to the challenge. He had no inkling how things would turn out in Nashville. He didn't know if the country musicians would accept him personally or find a way to enhance his particular brand of rock 'n' roll. But he realized that he had to try to go beyond the blues-rock sound of "Like a Rolling Stone." That song had to serve as merely a starting point in his evolution in electric music. Dylan needed to thrust himself into a daring new situation, if only to test himself and force his artistry to remain vibrant.

The gambit paid off brilliantly, confirming once again the wisdom of following your instincts. Dylan found himself so turned on by his new surroundings that he eventually recorded enough new songs to fill a two-record set, something unheard of before in rock 'n' roll. The bean counters were thrilled by the album's popularity. *Blonde on Blonde*, the product of Dylan's excursions in Nashville in the winter of 1966, is universally acknowledged to be one of his best albums to date. It reached number nine on the lists of the greatest albums of all time compiled by *Rolling Stone* and VH1, and eventually reached the double-platinum status for sales.

Leaving your comfort zone requires tremendous confidence. Sometimes the outside opinions that you've always trusted can prove to be shortsighted and misguided. In these situations, you have to think completely for yourself and swim against the tide. People think they know best for you. They'd rather keep you in a box of their making to maintain control. To get to Nashville in the first place, Dylan had to overrule the authority figure that had looked after his business affairs. Even though Dylan's producer, Bob Johnston, thought a shift to Nashville would help further the artist's creative process, which had stalled momentarily in New York City, Dylan's strong-willed manager, Albert Grossman, who had signed Dylan up back in 1962, was dead set against the notion. Grossman was an overwhelming figure, full of bluster and business smarts. "Grossman came up to me," Johnston recalled, "and said, 'If you ever mention Nashville to Dylan again, you're gone,'" Dylan biographer Howard Sounes recounted in his book *Down the Highway*. But Dylan proved more savvy than Grossman. He recognized what was missing in his muse, and he accepted the artistic challenge.

Never-Ending Rejuvenation

By 1988, Dylan had a pretty efficient and uniform way of life. Every year or so, he recorded an album in the studio. He also hired a band and went out on the road and did a few dozen shows in the United States or the United Kingdom or Australia whenever the spirit moved him or he felt a need to do something to help goose record sales. It was a pretty cut-and-dried system and didn't make excessive demands on him. It sounds like a convenient way to live, doesn't it? This was Dylan's version of coming to the office, punching a clock, putting in the time till he was ready to go home, and then repeating the process the following morning. The system proved, however, to be his undoing.

This almost decade-long routine nearly destroyed Dylan's art. Dylan has always defined himself first as a performer and then second as someone who wrote songs, made albums, gave interviews, counted his money, and lived the jet-set rock 'n' roll life. The fun and the challenge of working as a creative spirit got sparked when he got up in front of an audience and tested his limits. He loved honing his craft. If the audience dug it, that was terrific. What was more important to Dylan was that he was learning something every night, about his songs and himself.

Dylan knew that he wasn't putting himself on the line by touring every couple of years. When he contemplated the serious blues singers he so admired, the B. B. Kings of the world, he could barely hold his head up. They played upward of one hundred shows a year. On top of that, his record sales throughout the 1980s were subpar, save for such novelty albums as the in-concert release *Dylan & the Dead*, presenting songs from their 1987 series of shows in the United States, and the first recording of the supergroup the Traveling Wilburys in 1988. To protect his commercial and creative interests—what really amounted to the yin and yang of the music business for the participants—Dylan knew he had to shake things up. You know the feeling, too. You're not particularly challenging yourself in your craft. You do what is necessary to stay in the game, but you don't commit yourself to the work. You do just enough to maintain your status. Pretty soon, this second-rate dedication becomes a state of mind. It's lamentable because you're capable of so much more—and you know it.

"Up till then," Dylan wrote in his memoir about his perspective during the 1980s, "I had been kidding myself, exploiting whatever talent I had beyond the breaking point. I'd known it for a while. Recently, though, the picture had changed and now the historical implications of the situation bothered me."

Sensing that something had to give, Dylan quietly kicked off a series of concerts in California on June 7,

1988. He was backed by a stripped-down band, launching what puckish reporters came to label as the Never Ending Tour. He put himself back on the road and into new situations in which he had to prove his worth over and over again.

When the comfort zone that most of us work very hard to create for ourselves becomes stifling, it is important to take a page from the Dylan playbook. Instead of being lulled into complacency, why not shake up the status quo? Sign up for a new class, volunteer somewhere, put yourself in an unfamiliar situation, find a new job, challenge yourself to do something different. The possibilities are endless.

In most of the years from 1988 to 2011, Dylan performed roughly one hundred shows. His newfound vigor put him in front of different audiences and in venues ranging from the cavernous Madison Square Garden to quaint Minor League Baseball stadiums across the United States, requiring him to constantly adjust his performances and set lists. He was back to testing his limits, and that's exactly what he wanted.

Restlessness as a Way of Life

Stepping out of your comfort zone. On paper, it sounds quite enticing, doesn't it? This implies having freedom and derring-do and feeling liberated from the ordinary drill. For you and me, the idea might conjure up a daredevil activity, like skydiving or bungee jumping. In those pursuits, people seek to break out of the humdrum of their day-to-day lives. They suddenly embrace an adrenaline-charged moment or two that will leave them hanging on to a special memory, albeit one that has no connection to their real life, before retreating back to reality.

This is not what Dylan has in mind. When Dylan has broken out of his comfort zone, he has done it to achieve fulfillment, all right, but with the intent of doing something that will have a lasting consequence—not supply a momentary thrill. These are big-ticket risks that can change lives.

Many of us refrain from actively upending our lives. We don't want to take a gamble, because something might go wrong and put us behind the eight ball. Dylan, on the other hand, continuously puts pressure on himself to excel in every one of his highly public pursuits. These range from song writing to singing to recording to performing and even as far as creating artwork. From the outside looking in, we can conclude that Dylan must be an eternally restless person. Many of us have encountered someone who exhibits what is commonly called restless leg syndrome, someone who simply can't sit still and must continually jiggle his or her leg. I conjecture that Dylan has restless artist syndrome, because he can't stay in one creative place for too long. But Dylan employs his restlessness to achieve something productive.

When I throw around terms that I hope will come close to defining Dylan's essence, such as *reinvention*, what I am really saying is that the man always has an eye on the future and doesn't take much time to look back in either triumph or dismay. Where we might see a high risk, he instead envisions a tremendous opportunity wrapped inside of an adventure. Again, when nineteen-year-old Bobby Zimmerman dropped out of college, he didn't embark on a hippie quest to find himself. He knew exactly what he was—a folksinger—and he intended to pursue that vocation. Notice that I didn't write "his dream." Bob Dylan isn't by nature a daydreamer. He does things to get things done.

You can react in one of two ways when things feel stale. You can shrink and feel sorry for yourself, accepting your sad fate. Or you can take action to conquer those feelings, testing yourself, extending your reach, and challenging yourself to see both you and the world differently. It is ultimately up to you to take the responsibility for the unfolding chapters in your life.

For Dylan, who is his own harshest critic, the greatest measure of satisfaction stems from his penchant for throwing himself again and again into uncharted waters. It doesn't make much of a difference, either, if he is playing an old song or a new song or playing to a sellout crowd at a major venue or at a small-town theater. Nor does it visibly affect him all that much whether he draws standing ovations or catcalls night after night. What matters to Dylan is that he is constantly testing himself.

He is putting himself on the spot, always reaching beyond his comfort zone.

From observing Dylan's history, I dare to say that he is much more afraid of disappointing himself than of disappointing his audience. He places the burden squarely on himself to innovate.

Four

AIN'T NOBODY
LIKE DYLAN,
AIN'T NOBODY
LIKE YOU

What makes Bob Dylan so special? Sure, his treasure chest of great music is timeless. So, however, is artistry in any form. Therefore, it is not a big surprise that Dylan's vast catalog of brilliant lyrics and iconic vocals continues to remain in vogue from generation to generation. You're likely to hear someone playing "Blowin' in the Wind" on an acoustic guitar at a civil rights rally anywhere in the world. And your grandchildren will most likely glimpse someone singing it somewhere in fifty years, too. But what sets Dylan apart is bigger than his material, as great as it is.

Other musicians cover his songs all the time, but the minute you see him perform, you think, *That's Bob Dylan*. Instantly, the voice is recognizable as Dylan*'s*. He can sound alternately loud or quiet. For that matter, he can also appear contrite or defiant. It doesn't much matter what phase of life he is going through. He invariably sounds, for the lack of a dressier word, *real*.

What about you? What makes *you* seem real to those around you? When people in the office see you day after day, what do they think? Are you just "covering" someone else, or are you truly showing the original side of you? Most of the time, we don't make the effort. Either it is too difficult to pull off or there is too much inherent risk in revealing too much. But let me warn you: People can tell when you're going through the motions. The distinction between a show of devotion and the act of mailing it in can be profound. It's all up to us. Dylan tells us repeatedly in his lyrics that the key to success can be summarized by remaining true to your artistry, regardless of what you're undertaking either in an office or within a family. It's all up to you. Ain't nobody like Dylan, we think, in awe of his talents and accomplishments. Ain't nobody like you, he might tell us as if he were holding a life-size mirror right in front of our eyes.

What separates Dylan from other singers is this quality: We know exactly, unquestionably, who is behind the song. The answer, my friend, is really quite simple. Why has Dylan flourished in every musical incarnation in his life? He has remained an original throughout his journey. You can point to your favorite "Dylan." It can be folkie Bob or protest-writer Bob or rocking and rolling Bob or country Bob or gospel Bob or blues-singer Bob. Each one is totally valid. As we will see in this chapter, the quality of a person's voice can carry great meaning. What Dylan does literally with his—shaping it and using it to make strong points about himself and his life—you can do, too, with your aura. A voice is the essence of someone's individuality. And as Dylan shows us over and over again, individuality counts for everything when you assess the elusive goal of success.

It's the Singer, Not the Song

One of the great debates in rock 'n' roll annals is whether Dylan is a good or a bad singer. Some think he sounds like a dog whose hind leg is caught in a wire fence. The refrain of "Dylan can't sing!" has been heard again and again over time, from the release of his first album in 1962 to the reactions during his most recent tour. What nonsense! Clearly, Dylan has always been a commanding rock 'n' roll singer, who displays such emotion behind his words that he demands that people listen to him. Anyway, the debate simply doesn't matter to Dylan. He has always wanted to create a lasting impression on listeners, both on his records and in a concert hall. He expects them to remember his work.

Pursuing a reputation as an original can come at a price, naturally. Other people might very much like predictability because clones are easy to package and market to the public. They don't necessarily want or need someone who deliberately tries to sound like no one else.

In his song "Talkin' New York," one of his earliest folk tunes, he sang about the rough reception that some of the Greenwich Village club owners gave him when he auditioned for them in 1961. You had the impression that Dylan smiled inwardly when he remembered: "You sound like a hillbilly / We want folksingers here."

If the young and precocious Bob Dylan had ever paid attention to their rebukes, he didn't let on. Likely, he simply nodded his head respectfully at his elders and disregarded everything those shortsighted business people told him to do. They couldn't derail him from his desire to create something new. He intentionally carved out a niche of his own in the early days, while capriciously breaking all of the known ground rules of conduct for a proper Greenwich Village folksinger. Dylan well understood the hornet's nest that he was whipping up in the early 1960s when he dared to mix various accepted styles of folk music. What Dylan innately recognized was that the folk movement had no fixed identity, and he took advantage of the vacuum to insert himself in the vanguard of change.

"There was just a clique, you know," Dylan said in an interview with Cameron Crowe for his *Biograph* song collection. He continued:

> Folk music was a strict and rigid establishment. If you sang Southern Mountain Blues, you didn't sing Southern Mountain Ballads and you didn't sing City Blues. If you sang Texas cowboy songs, you didn't play English ballads. It was really pathetic. You just didn't. If you sang folk songs from the Thirties, you didn't do bluegrass tunes or Appalachian ballads. It was very strict. Everybody had their particular thing that they did. I didn't much ever pay attention to that. If I liked a song, I would just learn it and sing it the only way I could play it.

Read those words carefully: *"the only way I could play it."* There is no pretense about trying to fit in with what was standard operating procedure. Dylan teaches us a critical lesson in that remembrance. He tells us that he was proud to be different and that he strove for originality at all costs. Do you put yourself in what John Cusack's endearing and headstrong character Lloyd Dobler in the wonderful movie *Say Anything* termed a "dare-to-be-great situation"? Do you have the nerve to stand apart from everyone else and do things your way? If you bite your lip and mutter, "Nope," don't feel too badly about it. Not many of us do. But the ones among us who do have that intense drive tend to have a head start on success. Dylan had it in ample quantities.

The other lesson is that the best time to show your streak of individuality is exactly on day one. Dylan could have played the easy role of the pliable ingenue and gone along with the program of sticking to one style of folk music. He could have fit in nicely with his new older friends. He could have shown them the respect they believed they'd earned. But Dylan did it his own way from the get-go. It's much easier to start right than to change your attitude midstream. He certainly respected the knowledge of the more seasoned folksingers. But he saw that they didn't have the desire to break out of the mold. He did. And that made all the difference to him.

From One Original to Another

Bono, the lead singer of the great Irish rock 'n' roll band U2, understands what Dylan's all about. It takes, perhaps, a total original to understand the thought process of another one. Bono is nineteen years younger than Dylan and was raised in Dublin, a lifetime away from Hibbing. Nevertheless, Bono is a sensitive observer of the rock 'n' roll scene, and he plainly appreciates what Dylan accomplished by opening his mouth and letting it rip. More than anything else, Bono is in a position to acknowledge that Dylan has had an influence on his life and work, among the many musicians who faithfully followed Dylan. Bono used him as a blueprint and took it from there. To be lauded as a trailblazer is likely the highest form of praise that Dylan or anybody else in popular music could ever hope to receive.

"Bob Dylan did what very, very few singers ever do," Bono wrote in the pages of *Rolling Stone* when the magazine ranked the hundred greatest singers. "He changed popular singing. And we have been living in a world shaped by Dylan's singing ever since. Almost no one sings like Elvis Presley anymore. Hundreds try to sing like Dylan."

That is an insightful observation from a devout fellow traveler. More than engaging in mere glad-handing or celebrity backslapping, Bono is happily endorsing Dylan's eternal quest for originality and making it his own goal as well. Bono recognizes that Dylan is showing ample bravery, and he is giving the man props for it. "To understand Bob Dylan's impact as a singer, you have to imagine a word without Tom Waits, Bruce Springsteen, Eddie Vedder, Kurt Cobain, Lucinda Williams or any other vocalist with a cracked voice, dirt-bowl yelp or bluesy street howl," Bono continued in *Rolling Stone*. "It is a vast list."

Among the qualities you don't need is patience. It is anything but a virtue when you are anxious to forge a path all your own. You can't afford the luxury of waiting in line for your turn or standing passively till there's a break in the crowd. No, you have to barge into the scene. And you have to force others to make some room for you in the crowd, too. You can't apologize even once for displaying the characteristics of a bull in a china shop. Legendary New York Yankees owner George Steinbrenner used to have a plaque in his office that proclaimed, in the man's blustery fashion: "Lead, follow or get the hell out of the way." For his part, Dylan might brandish a sign that says simply and bluntly: "Get the hell out of the way."

"Here are some of the adjectives I have found myself using to describe that voice," Bono wrote, "howling, seducing, raging, indignant, jeering, imploring, begging, hectoring, confessing, keening, wailing, soothing, conversational, crooning. It is a voice like smoke, from cigar to incense, where it's full of wonder and worship."

If the qualities contradict themselves, very well, then, so be it. Dylan is all of those things and more. And so are you.

Bono is extolling, in describing Dylan's voice, the attributes of being your own person and respectfully thumbing your nose at an established mold. Bono—who has risen to the top of two very different fields, rock 'n' roll and philanthropy—knows how to push beyond the limits of one's public image. Think about that massive accomplishment. It also defies the imagination that the same bloke could master such diametrically opposed fields, such as the hurly-burly world of pop music and the community of billionaires. It is a triumph of chutzpah by someone who doesn't bow down to the establishment and does things on his own terms. If you asked Bono what kinds of qualities he possessed to make those strides, he might well point to Bob Dylan's. And he'd be spot-on, too.

Credibility Is Everything

Some of Dylan's best and most commercially viable music occurred when he went country in Nashville in 1969. The zenith of Dylan's crooning occurred on his ninth album, *Nashville Skyline*, which still stands as the calmest and most simplistic recording in his catalog. And you know what else it is? It is one of his very best creations. It is the work of a man who has originality pouring out of him. No less of a musical expert than Eric

Clapton called it a "very powerful" album when he spoke with Roger Gibbons of the *Telegraph* in 1987.

On *Nashville Skyline*, Dylan shows listeners that we don't have to be aggressive to be heard. We can leave our mark without shouting at someone. It's a lesson worth examining. Just as Dylan sounded entirely believable as the Angry Young Folksinger of Greenwich Village during the early 1960s protest-song movement, and America's Answer to the British Invasion a few years later, this chameleon also comes across as totally authentic by displaying a masterful grasp of country music. He makes it all his own. How does he do it?

How does a folkie turned rock 'n' roller reinvent himself to sound like someone who is standing a stone's throw from the Grand Ole Opry and has lived his whole life within the confines of the city limits of the 615 area code? What is Dylan teaching us here? His unspoken lesson is that we can be whomever or whatever we choose to be. It's all up to us. As long as we seem credible, people will accept us. Yes, Dylan, a highly skilled communicator based on his words and vocals, uses his music to leave his mark. But we can do the same in our own lives as well.

When you think about it in hindsight, Dylan took a sizable risk when he chose to morph into a latter-day Hank Williams on *Nashville Skyline*. All around him, his contemporaries were going in markedly other directions. In the late 1960s, the Beatles had been to India to meditate, and Dylan's spiritual twin John Lennon had become JohnandYoko. The Stones were sympathizing with the devil at Altamont. They were all writing songs with ominous-sounding titles like "Happiness Is a Warm Gun," "Cold Turkey," "Gimme Shelter," and "Let It Bleed." By comparison, Dylan was coming up with the likes of "Country Pie" and doing a duet with his pal Johnny Cash on the Mountain Dew theme song. But his gambit worked! He sounds totally unselfconscious in this laid-back style of music. This was clearly not a gimmick to him.

If you're going to create a new persona for yourself, you had better make sure you seem authentic to other people. There is a fine line between sincerity and parody, and onlookers always know when you're putting them on.

Like Dylan, you have to approach any new endeavor with complete commitment and respect. Anytime you do something new, people will be reevaluating you. If you believe in what you're doing, they will see it loud and clear. But if you're just going through the motions or acting out of cynicism, they will see that, too. People can recognize when you're acting like a phony or going for a cheap laugh or buck at their expense.

You Go Your Way and I'll Go Mine

Are you an original? Is that how people see you? Is that how you see yourself, for that matter? In your life, you, too, must strive to create a personal style that no one else could ever expect to replicate. When you've done that, you'll well on your way to fulfilling your goals.

Becoming an individual is not a temporary process. You need to carry it out throughout your life. You could argue that Dylan, in his advancing years, understands the concept even more profoundly than he did as a younger man. Discerning observers also grasp the point.

As ABC News pointed out when Dylan turned sixty years old:

> OK, so Dylan never had the greatest singing voice. But that's just it! That voice is what makes his words all that more powerful. The Byrds, the Band and countless other artists covering his work through the years may have made Dylan's words and music sound prettier, but those songs have their full power when the man himself is singing them, and blowing into the harmonica around his neck.

Or as Columbia Records succinctly put it when it built an advertising campaign around the release of Dylan's first greatest hits album back in 1967: "Nobody sings Dylan like Dylan." Dylan is an original, and so are you.

Yes, Dylan is an immensely talented and resourceful musician, singer, and songwriter. But what set his brilliant career in motion in the first place was his eagerness to take control of his life. Of all the lessons that we can take from his career, this is one of the most important, and it is something that everyone can take to heart.

Five

DON'T LOOK
BACK

B ob Dylan has uttered thousands of words in interviews since he launched his career in 1961. Come to think of it, maybe he has spoken tens or even hundreds of thousands of thought-provoking words along the way. My favorite Dylan quotation of all is only three words long. But it tells you just about everything you need to know about one of Dylan's core philosophies. What you should understand above all is that Dylan has lived out the sentiment expressed here, and it has led him to enjoy a life of success. This underscores the notion that you can start with a fundamental belief

in something and then apply it to everything you do—
and make it work brilliantly.

"Nostalgia is death," Dylan told interviewer Robert
Hilburn of the *Los Angeles Times* in a 1992 interview.
Whew! Those few well-chosen words pack the wallop of
a Mike Tyson right uppercut to the jaw. The expression
is at once blunt and profound. What moves me so much
about the phrase is that Dylan makes it clear to anyone
who listens to him that he refuses to be seduced by the
siren song of personal satisfaction at any pursuit. Taking
it one step further and applying it to our lives, it implies
that nobody should ever become too impressed with his
or her random accomplishments or legacy or, especially,
public image. As Dylan knows all too well, today's glow-
ing press clipping—"spokesman of a generation!"—can
be tomorrow's fish wrapping.

American singer and songwriter Josh Ritter articu-
lates what younger artists have taken from Dylan's
words. In a 2007 audio documentary, Ritter says,
"[Dylan] taught me a lot about not being satisfied with
what you've done, of not resting on what you've done
before, but pushing forward. If you ever arrive at a spot

where you're comfortable about [your music], rather than excited, maybe you're not doing it right."

Leave the Past Behind

Fans of Bob Dylan and film mavens alike know right away what I'm referring to with the title of this chapter. After D. A. Pennebaker filmed Bob Dylan's well-received May 1965 tour of the British Isles, he titled his documentary *Dont Look Back*, sans the apostrophe (though few people ever seem to remember to spell it correctly!). Pennebaker emphatically made his point with that evocative movie title. (In the interest of complete disclosure, let me remind you that the phrase itself is most commonly attributed to someone who has no visceral connection with either Pennebaker or Dylan. That would be the sage baseball pitching legend Satchel Paige, who once observed: "Don't look back—something might be gaining on you.")

Dylan can appreciate the sentiment. In his parlance,

we can point to his lifetime commitment to always looking ahead, a theme this book repeatedly drives home because it is central to Dylan's personal code. The Pennebaker documentary is a perfect example of it, too. It captures Dylan during his swan song to folk music. He never overtly said so, and his legion of rabid fans would have bitterly contested the point at the time. Although the 1965 Newport Folk Festival is usually hailed as Dylan's coming-out party as a rock 'n' roller, the genuine starting point occurred about six months earlier, when he recorded electric tracks for his *Bringing It All Back Home* album. He was drawing a line in the sand for his fans, his reviewers, his critics, and everyone else who cared about his music.

And that is a good example for all of us. It means that you shouldn't live in the past, either, that you should be excited about whatever lies ahead, and that you should embrace any fork in the road as well. It's the ultimate personal challenge to tell yourself that you will not live in the past and that you will actively break with the past so that you can fling yourself into the future. When we are defensive and defeated, we kid ourselves into accepting that we don't need to change anything in our lives. The unlucky ones among us trick ourselves into believing that we aren't getting stale. Ah, come on. Everyone does it at one time or another. But the smartest of us don't truly believe a word of our own blarney, and we feel an urge—no, make that a need—to test ourselves. If you're ambitious, you'll always push yourself, and the stiffer the test, the better you'll like it.

Why did Dylan have this fixation about leaving the past behind? As he has pointed out about the time, "I was making a nice living." He certainly felt no external prodding to change his style. In fact, the pressures on him were quite the opposite, in that many people wanted him to go *backward* and revert to playing, writing, and performing protest songs, instead of the more personal and surreal songs he was favoring at the time, in late 1964. The businesspeople hoped against hope that he would return to producing the kinds of compositions that originally catapulted him to stardom. That was their conception of Dylan, frozen in time. Forever. It was more than limiting. It was worse than stifling. It was positively destructive to his creative urges.

You may be nodding in recognition as you contemplate Dylan on the verge of his metamorphosis. Surely, you've been there, done that. You're in contact with people who just want you to stay the way you are. If you want to break with the past, you're on your own, like a complete unknown—okay, you see what I'm driving at. Why did Dylan sever ties with his own past and charge into the unknown? It's simple. He felt he had no choice. For Dylan, the phrase *don't look back* was a way of life.

Planned Abandonment

Perhaps more than anything, the secret to Dylan's success is his intuitive understanding that the past is the past. The key is knowing when to walk away—not just from failing enterprises but also from successful ones. It's hard enough to change when things are *not* working, but it takes true courage and determination to turn your back on something that is working fine at the moment. And yet, how many times has Dylan rejected a winning platform to pursue an uncertain future? How many of us can do the same?

A shining example, of course, is when he went electric in 1965, the decision that paved a path of unparalleled longevity and unimagined success. People called him a "fool" or a "traitor" as a result, but he knew the biggest career mistake is the tendency to hang on for dear life to things long past their prime.

Going electric may be the most visible example, but in big and small ways, Dylan has applied the concept of what management guru Peter Drucker called "planned abandonment" at many points throughout his career. According to Drucker, a necessary element of future success is the ability to walk away from current success. In other words, sometimes you have to stop one thing to start another.

In Dylan's many incarnations, we can see not only a beginning but also an end that propelled him forward to his next endeavor. Many times, it looked as if he had abandoned his music and sanity, not to mention his base of loyal fans, but you know what? He ultimately kept his fans, who by now have come to expect his ever-changing ways, and at the same time is being embraced by new followers who have discovered him during his last, seemingly irrational foray.

The concept of planned abandonment requires standing up to intense pressure designed to keep you stuck in the past. These pressures are everywhere and can become overpowering. They come from people, such as a boss or a rival who feels threatened by your talent and ambition. Or maybe it's a friend or family member who doesn't want you to get hurt so tells you to stay content with where you are. Mostly the voice that keeps us back is coming from within.

Even when—especially when—we feel we have made it, become successful, it's a useful idea to take stock and think about our next move. Dylan wrote at the tail end of his revealing memoir: "The folk music scene had been like a paradise that I had to leave, like Adam had to leave the garden. It was just too perfect."

When things are good is when you become complacent. It may sound as though Dylan is toying with his readers by applying some sort of backward logic. But on closer inspection, his sentiment makes perfect sense.

When he stresses that his folk music scene had become too perfect, he is telling us that he had reached the top of the mountain and it was then time to reevaluate everything. Dylan is reminding us how essential it is to continue to reach beyond our grasp. He points out that it is no fun to achieve what feels like a form of perfection if you then insist on staying stuck at that level of achievement. It makes you stagnant; you can't expect to grow that way. You can't imagine yourself surpassing your ambitions if you don't always attempt to view each accomplishment as a part of a long series of successes. Once you dwell for too long on one particular breakthrough, you're doomed to stay in that box. If, instead, you possess the capacity to recognize that you must build on your individual successes, you have fully embraced the meaning of "don't look back."

It's easy for any of us to get trapped by our own success. This pitfall can take place in any number of ways. It may seem like a paradox, but it is true, nonetheless, that the more accomplished you become, the harder it eventually becomes to resist complacency and continue to thrive. Staying focused is hard enough, but avoiding the pitfalls of day-to-day living is probably the toughest part.

Dylan understands the essence of the don't-look-back frame of mind: that if you're satisfied, the feeling is a shortcut to complacency. You're sunk once you sucker yourself into believing you have finished your journey because of some sort of achievement along the way. Dylan won't allow himself to be conned into thinking a feeling of accomplishment will automatically last forever. He knows whatever success he has enjoyed is only temporary, as if it were something on a string that could be pulled back at any time.

When Dylan Went Along to Get Along

Dylan didn't always follow his instincts, and he regretted it. Sometimes the pressure to bend is too great. When it came time for him to lay down the tracks to his first album, he should have followed the don't-look-back code and sung his own compositions. That way, he would have established himself right off the bat as a new, original voice. But he felt he had little choice. The prevailing notion was for singers making their first records to do tunes that were already accepted and well known. He was twenty years old, and he went with the flow, all right. That was in the fall of 1961, when he recorded his self-titled debut album on Columbia Records. Bob Dylan was then an utter novice. His producer, John Hammond, who had discovered him and then gone on to produce the first album, instructed Dylan to play the covers he had been performing in New York City nightclubs up to that point. Thus, the first album—which was highly influential to other young folksingers—was chock-full of songs that other artists had written. Dylan promptly disowned the record, as he said in the documentary *No Direction Home*. More than forty years later, as he talked about his first album, the contempt in his voice is still clear. But once Dylan discovered his lyrical voice, it's safe to say he did things his way for the rest of his life.

"Don't look back" doesn't mean *never* look back. One

of the most prominent examples of Dylan indulging in nostalgia—as well as a spectacularly successful case— took place on August 1, 1971, at George Harrison's historic Concert for Bangladesh at Madison Square Garden, in New York City. Harrison, who had made a pilgrimage to visit Dylan in Woodstock in 1968 as well as a visit to record some songs with him in Manhattan in the spring of 1970, called on him to appear on the bill. Dylan would be in good company, along with Ringo Starr, Eric Clapton, Ravi Shankar, and Leon Russell. Together, they would play music—in the first benefit concert of its kind—to help raise money earmarked to fund the relief efforts for refugees from East Pakistan after the 1970 Bhola cyclone and for those who suffered atrocities during the Bangladesh Liberation War.

Harrison was thrilled when Dylan agreed to play at both the afternoon and the evening concerts at the Garden. Harrison had never fronted a band before. Nor had he ever had to address an audience at length, much less one featuring twenty thousand New York rock fans! For his part, Dylan hadn't appeared in his adopted hometown of Manhattan in well over three years, so his showing would be a major coup for Harrison's concert. Dylan was understandably nervous about his performance—though someone as naturally self-confident as him probably figured, deep down, he'd do a good job. He was also likely wary about the musical message he would be sending out to the rest of the world. He wanted to help Harrison, who had become a good friend of his by then. But he knew what it would be like when he took the stage along with two ex-Beatles and a former star of the band Cream. At its worst, it might resemble a reunion of aging hippies singing their golden oldies. When Harrison beseeched Dylan to play "Blowin' in the Wind"—which Dylan hadn't performed in seven years—Dylan immediately asked Harrison if he would be willing to play "I Want to Hold Your Hand." But as we all know, Dylan played "Blowin' in the Wind" at each show, along with several other of his standards, and the crowd went wild. Dylan stepped back in time and achieved a special triumph that would last for the rest of his career.

Dylan showed that rules could be broken, and it isn't always a terrible idea to revisit the past—just not too often and, of course, on your own terms.

The difference is that Dylan didn't allow himself to be trapped by the past. He made what amounted to a quick pit stop, refueled, and got back into the (rat) race. If anything, he burnished his reputation by making those forty thousand rock fans so happy in the two shows at Madison Square Garden.

Dylan's point in doing the Concert for Bangladesh is that it's okay to honor your past achievements, as long as you don't succumb to the temptation of becoming a nostalgia act. There is nothing inherently wrong with making people happy every once in a while by fulfilling their expectations of you. It is significant that Dylan didn't play "Blowin' in the Wind" on stage again until the late stages of his Tour '74 engagements with the Band in tow.

In your life, you're expected to play a certain role, too, right? People have expectations of how we're going to act in different situations. There is a constant push-pull when we want to break out of the box and be someone different from what others demand. Just as it is vitally important to keep moving forward and breaking new ground, it is also fine to temporarily revert to what we used to be, as Dylan heroically did at the Concert for Bangladesh.

You don't have to turn into a novelty act. You can remain true to yourself by pleasing people, just for the sheer joy you know they're receiving. We're only human. It's a nice feeling to play a part when you know it will make other people feel happy, isn't it? Many of us dread school or family reunions because we're uncomfortable about having to live up to everyone else's memories and expectations of us. But Dylan showed that it can be rewarding to put on the old clothes, just once, and step back in time. And for the record, Dylan did attend his tenth high school reunion up in Hibbing, Minnesota, back on August 2, 1969. He even took the time to sign autographs, just to be nice. And that is a pretty high ideal in itself.

COLLABORATE
TO INNOVATE

Forget about his lifetime of remarkable accomplishments, his wealth, his fame, his awards, and his peerless legacy. Disregard, too, his hit records and sell-out tours, and the public's adulation to boot. Despite everything he has achieved, Dylan inevitably reaches occasional low points when he feels bereft of inspiration and motivation. When he hits bottom, he frets that he has momentarily lost his fastball. He faces the challenge of finding the will and the ingenuity to come up with another winning pitch. It's not easy to do. For a time, it's inevitable to give the appearance of coasting on a body of rich past glories. And it's dispiriting for

Dylan to take a look around at the scene and notice that young rivals, who have flourished largely by observing him closely and then following his lead, threaten to replace him as the crowd favorite and the media's darling. For a split second, as his illusions come crashing down around him, even Bob Dylan can't strike this gloomy question from his mind: Am I over the hill? After all, this can happen to anyone.

Doesn't that scenario sound familiar? In this respect, Dylan is no different from you or me. We all go through periods of extreme self-doubt. I worry whether I am useless to the people in my life. I wonder if they have noticed my deterioration. Maybe they, too, conclude that I am slipping. Or perhaps they have better things to think about in their own lives. It reminds me of the wonderfully incisive Albert Brooks line in the 1987 movie *Broadcast News*, when he says, "Wouldn't this be a great world if insecurity and desperation made us more attractive?"

What makes Dylan extraordinary—and enables him to come back from perceived failures and disappointments—is that he makes a point of not letting insecurity and desperation overwhelm him. One of the keys to Dylan's ability to enjoy longevity is that he finds solutions whenever he encounters a dark period. He doesn't mope around and feel sorry for himself or blame his woes on other people. He solves problems. It's ironic that people don't give him more credit for having this knack. People shower praise on him for his successes, but they seldom take the time to analyze exactly how Dylan manages to enjoy new triumphs.

Invariably, Dylan employs a method that is rather common in the world of mainstream business: He finds partners as a way to regain his muse. Sometimes you just can't go it alone. Sometimes we all need to tap someone either near and dear or new to give us a hand. Dylan shrewdly entered into a number of musical partnerships with people he could trust, who, whether they knew it or not, nurtured him. It may sound incongruous to us that a huge star like Bob Dylan could ever require nurturing. But when you abjectly lose hope in yourself and emotionally hit rock bottom, you most definitely need a boost.

Video Couldn't Kill
This Radio Star

When it comes to profiting from a partnership, Dylan could present a case study to Harvard Business School students about how he adapted to meet the demands of the MTV generation of the 1980s. The cable-television channel, which launched in 1981, almost immediately became recognized in the music industry as the most profound marketing innovation since FM radio. Suddenly, prospective record buyers could see newer stars, such as Madonna, Prince, and the Cars, singing their hit songs on television instead of merely listening to them on the radio, like their parents and other old fogies had always done. While MTV represented new opportunities, rock 'n' roll's old guard—including Bob Dylan—had to face the challenge of adjusting quickly to the new medium or lose out to the new wave of young, photogenic, and video-savvy recording stars. Trouble was, Dylan initially couldn't, or just stubbornly wouldn't, get behind the medium. Overnight, anyone who didn't appear prominently on MTV seemed, to the video-obsessed music industry and the audience alike, to be hopeless and hopelessly mired in the past.

"Hopelessly mired in the past." As you pondered that sentiment, you may have found yourself coughing or blinking or frowning because this doleful scenario may have struck close to home. Admit it. Dylan's predicament resonated with you, too. And if it didn't just now, well, trust me on this point: It will, sooner or later—and probably sooner.

We all go through it in one way or another. This is a function of finding your way in a competitive world, for as they say, what goes up, must come down. If you're a journalist like me, then the sobering fact is that when it comes to judging my relative value, I'm only as good as my last story or, to be even more blunt, my next one. Likewise, if you are a lawyer, you are only as good as the result of the last case you argued. The point is that it doesn't really matter what industry you work in. Everyone is vulnerable when a major change, such as a technological marvel like MTV, comes along. Just ask America's media industry in the late twentieth century. It was painfully slow to figure out that the Internet could be its friend and was much more than the latest gizmo to come down the pike. The message is always the same: Change or die.

"Dylan was an older artist, who was not of the moment," recalled Stuart Cohn, a lifelong fan, who joined MTV as a writer-producer not long after its debut in 1981. As he was speaking, he paused to smile, as if something had just jogged his memory. Cohn immediately added, "One afternoon, I was sitting in my office and listening to *John Wesley Harding*," an iconic Dylan album from 1967. Then, one of Cohn's young colleagues poked his head in and said, "Listening to music from the old days, eh?" Music from the old days didn't translate well to the video art form. Tellingly, when Columbia Records tried to break out Dylan's first post-MTV album, *Infidels*, in 1983, the label's first attempt at a Dylan music video—for his love song "Sweetheart Like You"—went nowhere. When Columbia insisted on another song from the album to be presented to MTV, Dylan found himself at a crucial point in the music video revolution.

Instead of looking for help from the music industry, Dylan knew he needed a fresh eye. He knew he needed to be pushed. Enter ebullient and brilliant Madison Avenue icon George Lois, who had the foresight to pioneer the use of sports stars in television commercials in the 1960s and create the memorable covers for *Esquire* magazine during that decade. Lois could be irascible, tough to please, and forceful. In other words, he was just what Dylan needed in a partner. Dylan could count on Lois to have creative ideas and light a fire under him.

"Bob, you have to fucking concentrate," Lois told Dylan when they got down to the business of having Dylan work on the vocals for the video of the song "Jokerman," the kick-off track from the uneven *Infidels* album. Lois had taken art prints from his home collection, featuring works by Michelangelo, Dürer, Munch, and, in an ironic twist, a Hieronymous Bosch painting titled *The Musician's Hell*. As *Rolling Stone*'s Kurt Loder pointed out in a piece describing the film shoot: "Lois' innovative concept was to superimpose the song's apocalyptic lyrics over the images throughout the video." But

Lois recalled how he had problems getting his distracted star to cooperate. "He's looking at me like, 'Uh-oh,'" Lois told me when I interviewed him in his Greenwich Village home in the spring of 2011. "I had to tell him, 'I'm locking the fucking door to the studio until you finish this fucking thing!'" Even then, Dylan came up with an artistic touch that conveyed ample sincerity and authenticity to the video. "He kept his eyes closed as he sang the song," Lois told me animatedly. "The crew was very annoyed. I loved it! He was singing to himself." Finally, Dylan finished his assignment. "He hugged me and was gone."

Dylan would have probably preferred to undergo a root canal than be trapped in a video studio. He could have found someone to coddle him and make the experience more comfortable, but that wasn't what he needed. Sometimes, the best collaborations work because one partner isn't afraid to press the buttons of a reluctant, otherwise highly successful colleague. What he'd needed all along was someone to challenge him and give him fresh ideas.

Jungle of Vines

One of the most profound examples of Bob Dylan benefiting from a collaboration resulted from one of his briefest partnerships, which shows that even a fleeting association can produce big dividends. This collaboration was the six-show engagement that he did with the Grateful Dead when they filled American football stadiums from coast to coast during the summer of 1987.

Dylan entered into the alliance with the Dead because he smelled a unique artistic challenge and a quick payday. Dylan and the Dead would play before some four hundred thousand people on that tour; at his usual pace, he'd have to play more than eighty concerts on his own to reach that number of spectators. He also needed a boost. As he wrote in his memoirs about his state of mind when he teamed with the Dead: "Always prolific but never exact, too many distractions had turned my musical path into a jungle of vines." Dylan wrote that in *Chronicles: Volume One*, revealing exactly how far he had sunk during the 1980s. Clearly, he needed a shot of inspiration from people who thrived on the challenge night after night of pleasing concert audiences. Well, say this for Dylan: As down as he was, he went to the right source. By then, the Dead was riding high like never before. The group had just released the hit song "Touch of Grey," a catchy, bouncing tune about acceptance of the aging process (accompanied by a terrific MTV-favored video!). Dylan wanted the Dead to help him fill seats—and make big bucks—and find a way to have fun. Buttressed by the star power of his newest bandmates, Tom Petty and the Heartbreakers, Dylan, indeed, got himself booked to play at big halls and stadiums all over the world throughout 1986. But he recognized the bitter truth. He had, by his own admission (as he wrote in his memoirs), lost all of the impetus to perform many of his old songs on stage. He had basically lost interest in being "Bob Dylan," a working musician who loved playing and singing his songs in concerts before thousands of people. He had surrendered his muse and desperately wanted to reclaim his love of making music and magic before it was too late.

As it turned out, audiences had mixed reactions to the curious pairing of two superstars from different sides of the rock 'n' roll tracks. I saw the first show on the tour, in Foxboro, Massachusetts, on the Fourth of July, and enjoyed the performance. I was thrilled to see Dylan on stage, the first time I'd caught him live since 1978. Mostly, I remember it as an uneven show, with some musical high points and a few disjointed renditions as well. Regardless of what I or any of the other critics thought, however, one person greatly benefited from this pairing: Bob Dylan. As Dylan wrote in his memoir, the teaming profoundly influenced him for the rest of his career. It gave him a sense of purpose that had been missing from his performances for years.

Dylan turned out to have a career-altering experience along the way. Thanks to an experience he had while hanging out with the Dead, he rediscovered his love of creating music at a time when he sorely needed to find some inspiration. As he wrote in one of the more poignant episodes in his memoirs, he excused himself from a session with the Dead on their home turf in San Rafael, California, and meandered into a nearby nondescript bar. He ordered a gin and tonic and watched an unknown combo rehearsing when something clicked in his mind:

The singer reminded me of Billy Eckstine. He wasn't very forceful, but he didn't have to be; he was relaxed, but he sang with natural power. Suddenly and without warning, it was like the guy had an open window to my soul. It was like he was saying, "You should do it this way." All of a sudden, I understood something faster than I ever did before. I could feel how he worked at getting his power, what he was doing to get at it. I knew where the power was coming from and it wasn't his voice, though the voice brought me back sharply to myself. I used to do this thing, I'm thinking. It was a long time ago and it had been automatic. No one had ever taught me. This technique was so elemental, so simple and I'd forgotten. It was like I'd forgotten how to button my own pants. I wondered if I could still do it. I wanted at least to have a chance to try. If I could in any way get close to handling this technique, I could get off this marathon stunt ride.

If Dylan had walked that day in a different direction, he might never have stumbled across the singer, who unwittingly showed him how to enjoy making music again. Sometimes the lasting effect from a collaboration isn't direct. Just being somewhere out of your usual element can put you in a different frame of mind and make you more open to new ideas.

Dylan's collaboration with the Dead left him with a renewed sense of purpose as he redefined his approach to making music, especially in concert. It's no coincidence that the following year Dylan launched the so-called Never Ending Tour, on which he has doggedly played one hundred concerts a year. By watching fans follow the Dead from city to city, he realized that he could attract a following in secondary cities and venues.

This partnership also afforded Dylan a friendship with Jerry Garcia—who died at the age of fifty-three of a heart attack in his sleep on August 9, 1995—as well as a rich collaboration with the Dead's stylish lyricist, Robert Hunter. "Garcia's attitude was that you just had to serve the music—and that everything else was bullshit," the Dead's biographer, Dennis McIntyre, told me in an interview, "and Dylan learned that lesson from Jerry."

We can see how much Garcia meant to Dylan. Consider that Dylan, who shied away from making public appearances of any kind, went to northern California and attended Garcia's funeral, to the surprise of many of Garcia's appreciative inner circle. "I was the doorman at the funeral, and I was shocked to see him, even though I had heard he'd be coming," McIntyre told me. As much as anything else, Dylan was saying thank you and bidding a fond farewell to the giant whom he had lovingly called his musical "big brother."

Tough Truths, Tough Love

There are times when tough love is not only the last resort but the smartest course of action—times when you are so bereft of motivation that a kind word would just be a waste of time for all concerned. Instead, what you require is a sharp poke, a prod, a kick, a shove, anything to knock you off your bearings. And I don't mean a heartfelt pat on the back. I'm talking about having someone, and it could be a stranger, shake you to the core, for your own good, and make you reexamine what you have been doing. Slowly, you'll begin to see where you have been coming up short. If you're lucky, you'll wind up asking more of yourself. It's not a natural thing for a person who is already rich, famous, and highly accomplished to seek out help from someone who is less decorated in a given field. This process isn't easy on your ego, to be sure. It isn't fun to have somebody inform you, repeatedly, that you need to step up and do better. But damn it, it can help you deliver the goods, all right.

This is the kind of reinforcement that Bob Dylan badly needed by the tail end of the 1980s. During that decade, Dylan had amassed a prodigious output. He released nine albums of entirely fresh studio and in-concert music. But outside of a moving set of lyrics here or a passionate vocal there, the subpar 1980s releases didn't come close to generating the kinds of sparks that Dylan had been known for in the previous twenty years.

Fittingly, the two 1980s albums that had enjoyed the biggest buzzes, showcasing Dylan, were his 1988 collaborative Traveling Wilburys work, with fellow rock superstars George Harrison, Roy Orbison, Tom Petty, and Jeff Lynne, as well as the 1985 three-CD collection *Biograph*, a glorified greatest-hits set containing many wonderful unreleased songs from over the years. As Dylan contemplated his final album of the decade, he sought out producer and fellow guitarist Daniel Lanois. Lanois had built an impressive résumé in recent years, successfully producing albums for such stars as U2, Peter Gabriel, and Dylan's former collaborator, the Band's guitarist and songwriter Robbie Robertson.

Very quickly, Dylan found out that Lanois had a strong will of his own.

To his credit, Lanois, who hailed from the Toronto area, was utterly unafraid to make Dylan think more about and work harder on this album than he might have under other circumstances. Sometimes tough love is the best kind of love—and an appropriate antidote for an individual who has been coasting on his or her laurels for far too long.

Dylan noted in his memoir: "I felt done for, an empty burned-out wreck. Too much static in my head and I couldn't dump the stuff. Whatever I am, I'm a '60s troubadour, a folk-rock relic, a wordsmith from bygone days, a fictitious head of state from a place nobody knows. I'm in the bottomless pit of cultural oblivion. You name it. I can't shake it."

Lanois became Dylan's self-appointed motivator, disruptor, and coach. Who's yours? You don't need a chorus, but it's important to have one person you respect and trust for straight answers. Someone to push you to meet your goals. Dylan, a musical superstar, required input from someone like Lanois, who was not afraid to speak his mind. They clashed to the point that Dylan wrote in *Chronicles* of feeling the need to ask his producer, "Danny, are we still friends?"

The dynamic, sometimes prickly, producer prodded Dylan from his cocoon. Lanois was just what Dylan needed to shake the cobwebs from his mind. He did anything but coddle his megastar singer and guitarist. Writing in *Chronicles*, Dylan explained why his partnership with Lanois, which resulted in the well-received 1989 album *Oh Mercy* and such fine outtakes as "Dignity," ultimately worked so fruitfully: "Danny was struggling to help me make this song work and he had the confidence to try anything. He cared a lot. Sometimes, I thought he cared too much. He would have done anything to make a song work—empty the pans, wash dishes, sweep the floors. It didn't matter. All that mattered to him was getting that certain something and I understand that."

Shelter from the Storm

As Dylan has demonstrated, you can never be too important (or self-important, for that matter) to seek help. There are times when you need to find someone who can lift your spirits and point you in the right direction. You may think it requires that you swallow your pride and admit a weakness. Not so. It is certainly no disgrace to reach out. On the contrary, it's a sign of strength to recognize that you can't go it alone all the time. When your life is most fulfilling, I would argue, it is a collaborative process.

Dylan clearly understands the point. He felt empowered by his encounter with the anonymous bar singer in San Rafael, California. He gained direction from his friendship and partnership with the Dead's Jerry Garcia. And he got a kick in the butt from music producer Daniel Lanois, who didn't back down, even when he worked closely with Dylan in the recording studio and had to exert his will over the often-contentious proceedings.

These are situations that we can relate to. You might see somebody on the subway, a stranger who exudes an unmistakable air of contentment that will remind you of the joy of living a happy life. Or you could get fulfillment from one of your professional peers, who can remind you why you decided to pursue your craft, way back when, in the first place. And yes, even if someone prods and pushes you—and even makes the workplace occasionally very uncomfortable for you—this is tough love can produce a profoundly successful experience.

Inspiration, we can see from Dylan's examples, can come from anyone, anywhere.

Bob Dylan faced dark periods throughout his career, but he managed to regroup each time. He found a way to come out of the darkness and discover the light. He did it with a little help from his friends.

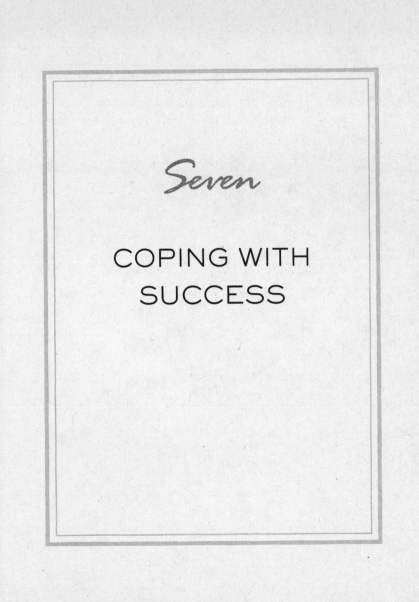

Seven

COPING WITH
SUCCESS

As Bob Dylan discovered at various points during his career, success can be quite complex. There is no manual for handling it correctly; it comes strictly from on-the-job training and an unscientific process of trial and error. It can seem like a vicious circle, too. When our accomplishments beget expectations, ours as well as those of other people, we can begin to feel tension and lose focus. Expectations, in turn, cause stress. This stress ultimately produces anxiety—and before we know it, we're cursing our hard-earned satisfaction instead of enjoying it. And it doesn't matter, either, how cool our friends and colleagues continue to tell us that we are. In fact, the more accomplished they gush we have become, the more we need to live up to. Ultimately, these pressures become oppressive.

Right before our eyes, everything changes. What had once seemed like some kind of an impossible dream—achieving a measure of affluence and recognition—can, instead, feel overwhelming. It's even more profound when someone attains a large scale of fame and fortune on top of it all. Eventually, this morphs into an unwelcome burden. And then what becomes of us? What can we do when "be careful what you wish for" goes from being a cautionary tale to our actual way of life? How well we handle a sudden rush of success can define us. There is, alas, no pamphlet for handling the strain that comes from a rush of wealth and fame. We imagine that successful people are sitting on top of the world when, in fact, they're struggling mightily to live up to expectations.

Whither Dylan? Just as he has shrewdly constructed a strategy for attaining success—by learning how to play folk music for a time in the outpost of the Twin Cities, before graduating to the mecca of Greenwich Village and taking the town by storm—he has also demonstrated how to survive the effects of it. Whether you want to chalk Dylan's durability up to his intelligence, self-discipline, or good fortune, it helped him dodge becoming a rock 'n' roll casualty, who choked on the excesses and numerous temptations, like Jimi Hendrix, Janis Joplin, Jim Morrison, Amy Winehouse, and Whitney Houston. On many occasions, Dylan has experienced the kind of massive strain that idolatry—on an out-of-control, almost unimaginable scale—can produce. "When he is recognized, it's every five steps," drummer David Kemper said (in a 2007 audio documentary about Dylan's life and career) of the crowd that invariably follows him around from town to town.

He has withstood the cauldron of public adulation by finding inventive ways of dealing with the tumult that is constantly swirling around him. More often than not, he has done what comes naturally: fall back on his love of writing and playing music, and use it to help him keep a sense of proportion. Dylan felt the bittersweet tug of success primarily at three points in his long career: first, when he became the king of folk music in the early 1960s; second, a few years later, when he crossed over to the rock 'n' roll scene and enjoyed massive praise for "Like a Rolling Stone"; and finally, in the 1980s, when he needed to mount a comeback and prove his relevance. Thanks to his muse, Dylan could achieve the best of all worlds: professional satisfaction as well as personal fulfillment.

You Have to Please Yourself

Bob Dylan could teach us plenty about coping with the pressures of stardom, especially the overnight variety. He was barely out of his teens when he wrote his first major song, "Blowin' in the Wind," in the spring of 1962. It immediately became an anthem of the twentieth century, and beyond. Although we can't expect to enjoy that brand of mammoth success, we can certainly take note of and appreciate exactly how Dylan has maintained his emotional and physical equilibrium in the face of tremendous pressures over a fifty-year cycle. Dylan has gone through, albeit on a massive scale, what a lot of us experience in our day-to-day lives and careers. How do you deal with the adjustment of being hailed as a star in your workplace or family or circle of friends? How do you act (or react) when it seems that everybody wants to bask in your glow and, more intrusively, wants something from you—whether it is love, advice, money, or attention? The same people who once needed only to joke around and hang out with you now require something from you. When everyone is telling you what they think you want to hear, it's very hard to know who your real friends are. The stress of sudden stardom was taking a huge toll on Dylan's central nervous system. "I'm going through bad times," Dylan told friends at around that time, according to Anthony Scaduto's biography *Bob Dylan*. "It's blowin' my head."

His solution was at once novel and practical: He focused on pleasing himself and let the chips fall where they may with his fans, peers, and business associates. He showed a facility throughout his career for following his muse and not kowtowing to what the suits or the audience demanded of him. He demonstrated again and again the value of keeping your own conscious, if only to allow yourself to take charge of your destiny. Even though Dylan is one of the most famous and accomplished people on the planet, his particular burdens are not so different, in theory, than yours or mine. Dylan has an occupation that places unique demands on him—so do you. Dylan has to keep the customer satisfied, as Paul Simon once put it—and you do as well. Dylan has to strike a balance between his public and private lives— and don't you identify with that predicament? It all comes down to how well you can cope with your own success.

Have you felt that way, when your success is squeezing you and making you feel isolated? Perhaps you, too, have felt like a prisoner of it. Success can be debilitating for all sorts of reasons. Once you've proven you can excel at doing one task, the odds are good that your bosses will continue to press you to keep on doing it, making it difficult to break out of your pattern and take on new assignments. Have your superiors ever pigeonholed you and made it tough for you to break out of their image of you? When this occurs, it becomes very difficult to grow. If you've felt the brunt of this treatment, you've probably failed to get hired or transferred or promoted because people want to keep you where you are. It's discouraging, to say the least.

Another by-product is imagining how the people in your life now regard you. Even if you struggle to remain the same, they look at you differently, perhaps suspiciously, because you have exceeded their own expectations. It can be extremely hard to change your image when people are content for you to stay in your box and continue performing the exact same functions in the exact same ways. The sad fact is that we live in a bureaucracy, and people don't usually have much imagination or sense of adventure, and you can get caught in the mill. But you can't let other people measure your value. You can't wait for the powers that be or the public to give you the opportunity to change and grow when they can't see anything that isn't right in front of their faces. It's up to you to seize the moment and show people what you can do. Not many of us are willing to do this. We feel paralyzed by fear and are reluctant to risk disappointing the people we depend on for approval and a good life. This is a shame, but the solution is quite simple: If you believe you have what it takes to excel, just go for it.

Dylan showed us how to defeat this syndrome. Just observe what he went through. He was determined to shake the public's expectations for him after he had established himself as the darling of the counterculture in the early 1960s. He recognized that he needed to do something bold and unexpected on the next album in 1964. Pointedly, it was titled *Another Side of Bob Dylan*. Despite the giveaway title, the audience hoped and expected, once again, to hear his brand of protest music, such as "The Times They Are a-Changin'," "Blowin' in the Wind," and "Masters of War." He instead teased his listeners by opening his fourth album with the track "All I Really Want to Do." Instead of what had become his characteristic, blunt, clipped vocal style, he actually laughed and even yodeled on the song, making it clear that his fans were, indeed, getting another side of Bob Dylan.

Dylan refused to subscribe to society's image of him, and he took it on himself to change his reputation. As he often does, Dylan was making a larger point that went beyond the grooves of a record album: Fight like hell to avoid having to live up to someone else's image of your self-worth. No matter how successful you have become, you can alleviate the pressure by not taking yourself oh-so-seriously. Most crucial, when you are living inside of a pressure cooker, take a step back and think about what you can do to keep a sense of balance.

Take One Giant Step Back

Sometimes, the best solution is to stop—and step off the merry-go-round for a time. Dylan bravely walked away from the limelight at the peak of his popularity. By the start of 1967, Dylan badly needed to have a break from the madness that had engulfed him for the previous several years. Dylan discussed the burst of chaos with Scaduto in a 1971 interview: "The pressures were unbelievable. They were just something you can't imagine unless you go through them yourself. Man, they hurt so much."

Chances are you can relate to an experience in which when the people you've trusted seem intent on piling on the pressures till you feel as if you were going to reach your breaking point. With Dylan, as we look back, the responsibilities do seem formidable on many levels. Still only twenty-five years old at the dawn of 1967, he was then recovering from a broken neck he had suffered in a motorcycle wreck the previous summer. Before the accident, he had just completed a grueling work schedule. From 1964 to 1966, he had recorded four studio albums, including *Blonde on Blonde*, rock 'n' roll's first two-record set. Somehow, each of his new recordings topped his previous effort in terms of creativity, originality, and a sense of ambition—a special accomplishment, and a rather stressful one at that. He had also toured the world, proud to show off his new sound, only to be greeted by a chorus of boos from disillusioned fans everywhere. They loudly expressed their resentment for his decision to abandon folk music and go electric. He had also churned out a television special and his first book. In addition, Dylan had gotten married and had fathered his first child. With concerns about his health, career, and personal life, he encountered major challenges on all sides.

Understand, it was unimaginable that a pop star on Dylan's lofty level would retreat into seclusion. Dylan all but retired from the stage and had his management company cancel the sixty-five U.S. concerts that had been set up for the autumn of 1966, beginning with the cavernous Yale Bowl in New Haven. Dylan answered the demands on him by setting a new agenda. Put simply, Dylan took charge of his life. He informed Columbia Records that he wouldn't be doing yet another new album, and it was free to release *Bob Dylan's Greatest Hits*. He didn't go back into the studio to make a new album until the autumn of 1967. He quit touring, a profoundly rebellious decision in a business in which practitioners had always thought they had to be seen by the public as a way to continue selling their records and satisfy their restless egos. He even stopped granting interviews. He relaxed up in Woodstock, away from the craziness. What he did in this simple stroke was nothing less than revolutionary. He was, as usual, far ahead of his peers. Consider that when John Lennon celebrated his life out of the spotlight, in a terrific song called "Watching the Wheels," he did so thirteen years after Dylan stepped back.

This is one of the most difficult things any of us can do: take control of our lives and change our destinies. It seems so much easier to let someone else—a family member, a boss, a business manager, an agent, or a financial planner—make the tough decisions for us. Dylan had done that for years but decided, as he later said in a 1974 interview with *Rolling Stone*, that the "leeches" in his life had played a part in creating a vicious circle of stress for him.

Of course, we all don't have the financial wherewithal to retire from public life, as Dylan did. But the key takeaway here is that Dylan knew when it was time to retreat from the limelight and stop competing for a bit, as he recharged his batteries. This requires an enormous act of will—especially when everyone else judges you to be at the peak of your powers.

The people in your life are often urging you to keep firing on all cylinders, possibly because they need to ride on your coattails. And the act of taking yourself out of the spotlight, by your own volition, is an extremely wrenching move. Most successful people are achievement junkies. They thrive on competition and the satisfaction of winning. Success is most definitely a fantastic high and much more fulfilling than any drug. Most of us simply aren't strong enough to resist the siren song. It seems so much more natural to remain on the merry-go-round of life and continue doing what you have always done—even if you suspect, in your heart, that it is grinding you down, driving you crazy, or literally killing you.

Dylan also found refuge from the insanity in his family. We often read *Mommie Dearest*–type accounts, in which children feel their parents weren't there for them throughout their lives. It's especially acute when celebrities are involved because of the mammoth publicity they invariably receive from the gossipy media.

In Bob Dylan's case, however, there was none of that. In fact, I was struck by the outpouring of affection that Jesse Dylan, Bob Dylan's eldest son, had for his dad when I interviewed him for a MarketWatch piece that appeared on March 26, 2010. I had a feeling that Jesse and I would get around to talking about his father at some point, but I wanted to tread lightly because I knew from reading scores of books and speaking with people in Bob Dylan's circle that he was an intensely private man. I assumed that Jesse would also guard the family's privacy, and I wanted to respect his wishes. Still, I was curious to find out what I could.

My interview with Jesse Dylan occurred long before I ever had a contract to write this book. I had been intrigued by Jesse's commendable public service in Lybba, a nonprofit that sought to use social media to help bring together doctors, researchers, and patients to help improve the understanding of medicine. Inevitably, our conversation swung around to Jesse's influences and roots—and, sure enough, you-know-who popped into our conversation.

I suggested that Jesse was carrying on the good work in society that Bob Dylan had done so many years earlier with his galvanizing 1960s songs. As I wrote in my column, "While evidently flattered, Jesse said a comparison 'is not apt. I'm a translator. I take what other people are doing.'"

The affection that Jesse feels for his father came shining through during our conversation, which took place in the East Village of Manhattan, a stone's throw from where Jesse had attended New York University during the 1980s, and Bob Dylan had set the world on fire two decades earlier.

I had written in my column on Jesse Dylan: "One of Jesse's comments stuck with me, though. When I mentioned that I'd admired *Chronicles: Volume One*, Bob Dylan's acclaimed 2004 memoir, he nodded and said: 'He is an even better father than writer. He is my best friend.'"

Finding Fun Again

Dylan has had his ups and downs over the years, and his public persona has often reflected whether he is happy or not. In the 1960s, he was often photographed with a smile on his face. But two decades later, he came across as a rather rigid, severe individual, possibly because a lot of people still retained their late-1970s image of him as a born-again Christian. It can be very tough to shake a powerful media-fed image like that one.

As the decade wore on, the indelible image of the public Dylan was his erratic and bizarre performance at the monumental Live Aid benefit concert on July 13, 1985, in Philadelphia. Dylan was admittedly hampered by a faulty sound system and sabotaged by Keith Richards and Ron Wood of the Rolling Stones, who had joined Dylan on stage but seemed to be on another planet as they played backup guitar. Dylan simply looked out of synch.

In photos taken at the time, Dylan looked like a guy who wasn't having any fun. By his own admission in *Chronicles*, he was burned out, undermotivated, and disenchanted with the music industry. More likely, Dylan was just plain tired of pleasing people and had gone as far as he could go at that period. He needed to remember why he had decided to make music in the first place—for the fun of it and the sheer challenge of creating magic. You don't have to be a musician or any kind of an entertainer to understand what Dylan was experiencing.

I, for one, can relate to this kind of syndrome. Can't you? There are times when work feels like nothing more than drudgery. It's a job, not an adventure, and the fun and thrill of discovery are nowhere to be found.

When this happens, sometimes you just have to stop taking yourself so seriously. It's essential. You can't eliminate the pressure of doing a good job and winning acceptance, but you can decide to start having fun again. For a lot of us, the happiest times of our lives occurred when we found ways to whistle while we worked. We could laugh through the aggravation and tension of everyday life.

Dylan's answer was the Traveling Wilburys, an impromptu band of superstars put together in Los Angeles in the spring of 1988 by his good friend George Harrison. Harrison invited Jeff Lynne, formerly of the Electric Light Orchestra, Tom Petty, and Roy Orbison to join them, and the experience revitalized Dylan, primarily as a songwriter. He hadn't much tried his hand at creating songs with funny lyrics in that decade, but he came alive on this experimental album. He wrote "Congratulations," "Dirty World," and "Tweeter and the Monkey

Man," the latter two tunes being rich, clever homages (or send-ups) of Prince and Bruce Springsteen, respectively. The album turned out to be a big hit with critics and the public, thanks largely to Dylan's involvement. He benefited in turn, too, as it provided the spark for him to write the well-received songs on his next album, 1989's *Oh Mercy*. By dialing down the intensity button and learning to have fun, Dylan also learned a lesson. Now he can teach it to us.

Once we have made the big time, our first impulse may just be to sit back and soak up all of the applause and act as if the adulation were going to go on forever. Guess again. Life doesn't quite work that way. Once we've accomplished a goal, the pressure is on to maintain or exceed that sort of success again and again.

What Dylan shows us is that the key to handling success is not to let the pressure to excel swallow us up. The journey back to personal fulfillment can be the most rewarding part of our lives. How we go about recharging our batteries says a lot about us.

Eight

MARRY A
MERMAID

Observers of the pop culture scene have scrutinized Bob Dylan for decades and tried to explain his longevity. One word that pops up again and again is *genius*. But that answer, while acceptable, is nonetheless too pat, too easy, because the value of the word has been diluted through massive overuse. Dylan is complicated. He requires greater exploration than merely measuring his accomplishments, one by one, and pointing to each as the evidence of a remarkable legacy.

It's more valuable to identify the common thread in Dylan's approach to solving problems. We can start by pointing to his overriding commitment to doing a job well, creating a lasting impression on an audience, and leaving them wanting more. He does this by going, in the parlance of a poker champion, all in. That is, he throws all of his chips into the center of the pot, signifying that he is willing to risk everything he's got to meet his goal. He is going to force the action. He is going to make people take him seriously. He'll do whatever it takes to establish a persona all his own. To do this properly requires a strong sense of self, plus a highly developed imagination, with a sprinkling of chutzpah thrown into the mix for good measure.

Dylan simply sees the world differently from the way you and I do. His brain operates on a whole other level. Where others might ponder a certain challenge and carefully weigh the risks and rewards and calculate the probability of setback, Dylan doesn't even consider the possibility of failure. He doesn't take into account that there are boundaries or limitations to attaining success. It's a sign of Dylan being all in and not compromising himself. When we try to analyze Dylan's success, we can see, on one level, that it is more a factor of perspiration than inspiration. He throws himself completely into his various music, art, literary, and film projects. He intends to go deep and, in the evocative phrase he invoked in his memoirs, "marry a mermaid." It starts with the notion that he is committing himself 100 percent to everything he does.

What's in a Name? (Oh, Everything)

As we have discussed, Dylan has remained a man of action, making swift, decisive, life-changing moves. One of the most transformative acts of his career and life took place a half century ago, personifying his credo of dedicating himself completely to a task. The act centered on Dylan's decision to create a brand name for himself, a permanent identity that would take his career to a whole other level.

He came up with the stage name Bob Dylan while he was in college in Minneapolis circa 1959–1960. But he was still legally known by his birth name when he arrived in New York City. This would have to change if he wanted to carry off the legend of Bob Dylan. So, the Bob Dylan whom we know and love was actually born on August 2, 1962. On that fateful Thursday, he went to the Supreme Court building in lower Manhattan and changed his name from Robert Allen Zimmerman, which his loving parents, Abe and Beatty Zimmerman, had given him at birth, to Bob Dylan.

We take for granted the significance of that act. After all, it is common in show business for someone to change his or her name in the hope of coming up with a catchier moniker. But who had the cheek to pick the name Dylan, which conjured up images of the rough-and-tumble, hard-living poet Dylan Thomas? His new name was going to stick, all right. Remember this example when you are pondering a career move, and follow Dylan's approach of doing something so unexpected, so out-and-out daring, that you are guaranteed to leave a lasting impression. It works.

What single act in a person's life could more profoundly embody the concept of being all in than changing his or her name—especially when that person, as a promising young poet, has adopted a name best known as belonging to a legendary poet?

Dylan understood this and embraced his decision, knowing it was a way to reach out and touch his destiny. Consider that when Ed Bradley, the distinguished correspondent of CBS's newsmagazine *60 Minutes*, interviewed Dylan in November 2004, he specifically asked him why he changed his name back in 1962. Dylan said the move was clearly a part of his destiny. "Some people—you're born, you know, [with] the wrong names, wrong parents. I mean, that happens. You can call yourself what you want to call yourself. This is the land of the free." It should be noted here that Bob Dylan has never publicly confirmed that he took his name from Thomas.

It all comes back to knowing what you want to be and your level of ambition. It centers on forging a way for people to know and recognize you—and, yes, going all in, at the same time. Dylan wasn't likely to take the name Smith or Jones. Someone with his adventurous spirit would pick a name that made people pause and think. He teaches us here the value of putting ourselves on the line 100 percent. If you're going to do something, make a lasting impression on people. Leave them talking about you. Prompt them to want to know more about you. You don't have to change your name to create that effect, to be sure; Dylan shows us just how much someone can accomplish by having an adventurous spirit.

Go All In

If you were to poll Bob Dylan's longtime fans, many might say that the most shocking and unexpected chapter in his life took shape November 1, 1979. At 8:20 p.m., a compact black woman named Regina Havis bravely strode to the microphone at San Francisco's Warfield Theater to open Bob Dylan's first concert since the world learned earlier that year that he had become a born-again Christian.

The audience looked on in amazement. Who is this? And where was Dylan? Undeterred, Havis launched into a story about an old woman who wants to get on a train so she can visit her dying son but doesn't have the fare. The conductor refuses to let her on board. But the train won't leave the station without her. The man finally orders her to get on by saying, "Old woman, Jesus got your ticket."

Havis and her accompanying female singers performed six smoldering gospel numbers before Dylan walked purposefully on stage. Without saying so much as a word of introduction, he blasted right into "Gotta Serve Somebody," the single from his just-released album *Slow Train Coming*. His fourteen-concert stand in San Francisco was off and running.

Burning with the spirit of the convert, Dylan sang seventeen songs that night. To the audience's amazement, all of them were brand-new compositions, and every single one dealt directly with his special relationship to Jesus Christ. Not "how does it feel?" Not "how many roads must a man walk down?" Not "everybody must get stoned."

"All old things are passed away," he said from the stage in answer to calls for him to play "Lay Lady Lay" and other longtime favorites.

Reflecting the feeling of many in the crowd, Shasta, a Bay Area musician seated near the front of the auditorium, wondered, "What the hell is he doing?" A veteran of a half dozen Dylan concerts, Shasta was shocked by the spectacle. He recalled, "It was wild! You had the Jews for Jesus people out in front of the Warfield, handing out pamphlets with drawings of Dylan on the cover. On stage, I thought he looked like he was friggin' hypnotized by all these Jesus freaks."

A tremendous surge of anticipation had swept through the seventy-seven-year-old vaudeville-era concert hall. Neither the sell-out crowd of 2,250 nor the performer himself quite knew what to expect that evening. As he wrote in the liner notes to his *Biograph* collection, "[When] nothing is predictable and you're always out on the edge . . . anything can happen." He also acknowledged, "When people don't know what something is, they start to get, you know, weird and defensive."

But Bob Dylan's zeal to spread the gospel was more than an act. Dylan was on a mission, and the blessed critics be damned. Dylan doggedly played the same concert of all-Christian-faith music every night over the ensuing three weeks at the Warfield Theater.

Dylan wasn't blind to the dangers of presenting a show of all-new, fundamentalist Christian themes to an audience seated smack in the self-styled hippest city in the nation. Dylan gathered the troupe backstage before the gig and led them in a prayer group to prepare them for the possibility of a hostile reception. And yet he plowed onward. "He was," his then assistant Arthur Rosato said, "on a mission." Would you have the guts to follow your passion in the face of certain criticism? How many of us would call it quits before even starting?

It's no coincidence that this point in Dylan's life personified the total commitment to a cause. At the time, his new passion was an immense surprise—and not one that was easy for his universe to accept at first blush. He was on a path of self-discovery, and he wasn't going to be a half-measure man about it. He was risking the alienation of his fan base, a liberal-minded group that looked at born-again Christians in a narrow-minded way. It was certainly not the fan base you'd freely associate with Bob Dylan, who had championed leftist civil rights and antiwar platforms as a young songwriter. Ultimately, Dylan's born-again phase proved to be a valuable chapter in his career because it afforded him an opportunity to express himself in a way the public had never heard before and burnished his reputation as an independent-minded artist. Clearly, this chapter marked the ultimate act in fully investing himself to something.

Following the release of *Slow Train Coming*, he embarked on an ambitious series of concerts to spread the word of his spiritual beliefs. He even made an appearance on *Saturday Night Live* and sang three songs from *Slow Train Coming*, marking his first U.S. television spot in four years. That gesture alone told us that Dylan was gravely serious about his new direction. For someone as private as Dylan, he might well have dreaded the prospect of having to go on a national television show, aware that he was opening himself up to the ignorant naysayers' complaints and criticisms.

Dylan was appealing personally to a higher power. But we can take the sentiment of the passage one step further and project it back to principles that Dylan has always held close to his heart. As he sings, he is also affirming his drive and determination. This was true when he elbowed his way into the bosom of Greenwich Village's folk community with an unconventional musical approach. It was correct, too, when he hurtled himself into the rock 'n' roll scene a few years later. And it was also the case when he took his talents to Nashville to blend his sound with country music. He is telling us that he is committed to what he is doing, despite the public outcry against him.

When Dylan turned to Jesus for comfort, he knew he was taking a huge gamble with his popularity. Fans were confused and frightened by the latest incarnation of the new Dylan. Others perceived it more cynically. Ron Wood of the Rolling Stones joked that his bandmate Keith Richards had good-naturedly dubbed Dylan the new Prophet of Profit. "Yeah, I went to Santa Monica Civic to see him, as Keith says, in his 'Prophet of Profit' days," Wood told interviewer John Bauldie in 1988.

Every time you choose to make a radical, public change in your life, no matter who you may be, it may seem easier to try things halfway, to see how it will work out. But Dylan didn't just dabble; he went all in. Dylan acted like a man on a mission, critics be damned. It was important—critical—for Dylan to live his life the way he wanted to, without worrying about the repercussions. And when something matters that much, it can't be done halfway. You can't put your pinkie toe in the water. You have to dive in and, as Dylan says, "marry a mermaid."

Dive Deep

When Dylan agreed to host *Theme Time Radio Hour* in 2006, executives would have probably been satisfied if he just showed up. Certainly Lee Abrams, then head of programming for XM Satellite Radio, was thrilled just to have Dylan's name on the marquee. His competitor, Sirius, had poached Howard Stern from traditional radio. Who was going to anchor XM? One name kept coming up. Trouble was, no one seemed to have a clue as to how to get to Dylan. Abrams turned to XM supporter

Willie Nelson, as Abrams recalled in a lengthy blog post in April 2006, and noted that Nelson said, "I've been on the road with Bob for a month . . . and haven't seen him yet."

Abrams, borrowing a page from Dylan's playbook of persistence, didn't give up. When he finally found his way to Dylan's management, it took three days, according to Abrams, to finalize the deal. And as it turned out, Dylan had specific ideas on how to use this new medium.

XM staffers had expected to present Dylan with concepts for the show. Instead, he began bombarding them with concept questions and set lists. Even though hundreds of people were involved in producing the show, Dylan's imprint is in every detail, from the show's concept to set lists that sent music archivists scrambling. Fans knew they were being treated to something as unique as Dylan himself. Dylan's involvement set the standard for celebrity shows of its kind as he further helped put XM on the map with boomers, the well-heeled demographic that loves Dylan's music.

Even here, Dylan threw himself into what was really

just a side venture. It didn't require any earth-shaking changes. This was no Newport. But Dylan saw the potential to reach new and old fans in a unique way, while indulging in his love of the music of his boyhood. Plus, he was genuinely curious about this new medium. He wanted to learn and stretch himself, and by throwing himself completely into the challenge, he redefined the art form. To Dylan, being 100 percent committed doesn't mean "I'll try it out" or "I'll wait and see." Once he decides he's in, he's all in.

The Secret of Genius

Dylan's accomplishments stem from his ability to see the world in his unique manner. It is beyond irrelevant to him that people won't accept what he is doing or recognize the inherent value of his undertakings. It is absolutely meaningless for him to think in these debilitating terms because if he did, it would slow him down and sidetrack him. Instead, Dylan pushes on, immersing himself 100 percent in what he is doing. Dylan has a gift for writing songs, all right. But perhaps the true measure of his special genius is that he puts all of himself into his endeavors, never letting the prospect of defeat stop him in his tracks.

As one of the most famous and admired rock 'n' roll stars in the world, Dylan, again and again, has mustered the strength to defy the expectations of others to come up with something very personal and completely original. For all of the ballyhoo that rock 'n' roll stars are mavericks, the hard truth is that most of them stick to the tried-and-true, fearing a swift and merciless rejection by the ever-fickle audience.

It probably never dawned on Dylan that he might need a backup, just in case things in popular music didn't quite pan out for him. Failure was not an option. He bet solely on himself—it's what high achievers do, by design. They put themselves on the line; they want the responsibility; they place themselves in dare-to-be-great situations.

People like Dylan don't try to please others. They do things for themselves, raising the bar higher and higher to challenge themselves. They achieve satisfaction when they jump into the pool at the deep end. This is how they can see what they're made of. They don't sink—they swim.

Nine

LIVING BEYOND
OTHER PEOPLE'S
EXPECTATIONS

On April 12, 1963, Dylan marked a major turning point in his life during the most prestigious show of his career to date. It occurred at Town Hall in Midtown Manhattan.

Dylan's fans had embraced him as the continuation of the beloved songwriter and singer Woody Guthrie, America's mid-twentieth-century Dust Bowl poet laureate, who had penned "This Land Is Your Land" and many other classic Americana tunes.

That evening Dylan unexpectedly announced he was about to read something that he had recently written. Someone had asked him to contribute to a book about

Guthrie, he explained, and the assignment was, "What does Woody Guthrie mean to you in twenty-five words?" Pausing at the utter absurdity of the mindless question, Dylan noted he "couldn't do it. I wrote out five pages, and I have it here, have it here by accident, actually." If all of that wasn't enough of a jolt, he announced that the poem was called "Last Thoughts on Woody Guthrie." By coining that title, Dylan left nothing to chance for his audience. He wanted to hammer home the point that he was his own man and people had better accept him. The poem deals with one of the themes—the inequity between the haves and the have-nots in society—that Dylan frequently wrote and sang about in that period. In an example of the free-form series of rhymes of the poem, Dylan read, "And your minutes of sun turn to hours of storm . . . I never knew it would be this way, why didn't they tell me, the day I was born."

The poem itself mentions Guthrie's name for the first time in the final stanza, but Dylan's fellow musicians could easily grasp the significance of "Last Thoughts on Woody Guthrie." Eric Clapton told interviewer Roger Gibbons for the *Telegraph*, a publication devoted to all things Dylan, in 1987: "That to me is the sum of his life's work so far, whatever happens." Clapton elaborated on Dylan: "Basically, he's a poet. He does not trust his voice. He does not trust guitar-playing."

Dylan accomplished something that all successful people do, at one point or another: They decide that they are ready to step out of the long shadow of their mentors. In Dylan's case, it must have been an emotional decision, for Guthrie loomed large to him. In *No Direction Home*, the 2006 Martin Scorsese–helmed documentary, Dylan said he had traveled to the East Coast in 1961 expressly to visit Guthrie in a hospital in Morristown, New Jersey. Later that year, Dylan wrote and recorded for his first album the evocative tune "Song to Woody." In the late 1980s, in an interview in England, Dylan noted that in his youth in Minneapolis and Greenwich Village, he had been a "Woody Guthrie jukebox." But the time had arrived at Town Hall for Dylan to be his own man. It was a sign of his personal growth. He was bursting at the seams with self-confidence and burning with ambition to take his art in a new direction.

It underscored a deep-seated need for him to take command of his public persona and point to a new direction. He was telling people that he would never discredit the influence of Guthrie on his muse and his life. But he was now twenty-two years old, the age at which his peers were graduating from their college campuses and entering the real world. Dylan, too, was advancing in his quest to make it big as a singer and songwriter. He had matriculated at the University of Woody Guthrie and was now progressing to a new world as well. Even though he remained intensely loyal to Guthrie's legacy, Dylan recognized that he could no longer let music people and the society at large believe that he was primarily still an acolyte of Guthrie.

Dylan had gradually grown beyond the image of himself as the embodiment of Guthrie. He needed to tell the public that it had to adjust its perception of him. Dylan parted with the past in a respectful and smart manner. But his message was clear: Respectfully, folks, he all but explicitly told the throng at Town Hall, I am not the new Woody Guthrie any longer.

Think for Yourself

Dylan turned the biggest corner of his career when he started to write songs around 1961. Previously, he had exclusively sung the work of other songwriters, principally Guthrie. By coming up with his own tunes, Dylan was able to cut his ties with Guthrie and clearly establish his own voice.

This move enabled Dylan to put his stamp on the times and carve his own niche. The singer-songwriter is all too common nowadays, but in the early 1960s, the idea that a folksinger would write his or her own material was a fairly radical one because it was frowned on to thumb your nose at the musical standards. "Why would someone want to do *that*?" Ray Benson of the folkie singing group Asleep at the Wheel asked rhetorically on a 2007 disc tracing Dylan's long career. "There's so much good stuff out there already!" That was the sentiment when Dylan was trying to break into the folk music scene.

But Dylan knew better than anyone else that he had gone as far as he could by singing other songwriters' classics. He was ready to put his imprint on the folk world. Talk about a supremely empowering personal moment of liberation. It was as if the young and precocious Bob Dylan had declared to the rest of the folk music world, "I am ready to make my mark, and I want the others to start following me from now on."

By making the move to writing his own songs, Dylan was doing just that. For him, it was a moment to remember. As he wrote in *Chronicles*: "I can't say when it occurred to me to write my own songs. . . . I guess it happens by degrees. Sometimes you just want to do things your way, want to see for yourself what lies behind the misty curtain."

To truly become great, you have to step out of other people's vision and into your own. For Dylan, this meant writing his own songs, and the decision was a moment to cherish.

It boils down to how much you'll push yourself in the face of existing societal conventions. Have you ever done (or dared to do) anything comparable in your field to what Dylan pulled off? How do you go about pushing aside the expectations that weigh you down?

Sure, many people can tell you that you're on top of the world and that they admire and even envy you. That sort of praise can become intoxicating. But when you believe your own press clippings, you're on a fast track to self-destruction because you'll lose sight of what you know is important: blazing your path and thinking for yourself, instead of living up to the image that the outside world has constructed for you.

You need a strong backbone to tell your most fervent admirers that you are turning your back on their notions. Some will understand, some won't, and some will fight you every step of the way.

Yes, people are going to be surprised and, in many cases, archly critical of you. They'd rather keep you in the same place because if you grow and change, they'll have to shift their way of thinking about you. And as we know, most people do not welcome change in their lives because it can be stressful. And so what? Who cares if the people give you flak? You can't live your life simply to please the crowd. It's better to try to be a leader than a follower.

We hate to admit it, but we do contemplate prospective disappointments and rejections. These fine points certainly matter to us—and to our detriment. We all fret about looking foolish or getting criticized if we dare to do something unconventional or unpopular. It's human nature. But it also smacks of a frailty that can keep us from advancing and meeting our objectives. Fear makes us less certain of our ability to take on new responsibilities. Worrying about failing can be the biggest single factor preventing us from putting our best foot forward and charging into the fray.

Dylan has faced this crucible on more than one occasion, and any number of them would neatly provide a worthwhile example. But the case that shines through most prominently for me is when Dylan decided to expand his folk music repertoire and go beyond the kinds of protest songs that had made him a global phenomenon. Not many of us would have the guts—and there is really no other suitable word—to do what Dylan did in 1964, when he stopped composing finger-pointing songs, as he liked to call this style of songwriting, in which he made commentaries on the world around him and issued proclamations about injustice, race relations, politics, and tyrants. Instead, he would now write about what he was thinking and explore his own thoughts more deeply. He showed courage in openly going against the tide and doing what he wanted to do.

Dylan has made it clear that he had no interest in living out somebody else's vision of his way of life. "Whatever the counter culture was, I'd seen enough of it," he wrote tellingly in *Chronicle*. "I was sick of the way my lyrics had been extrapolated, their meanings subverted into polemics and that I had been anointed the Big Bubba of Rebellion, High Priest of Protest, the Czar of Dissent, the Duke of Disobedience, Leader of the Freeloaders, Kaiser of Apostasy, Archbishop of Anarchy, the Big Cheese."

Dylan set out to challenge himself and go beyond the brilliant bluntness of "The Times They Are a-Changin'" and songs of that ilk. He would now push himself to reinvent the language of the folk song. But as we can see, anyone who has the musical genius to come up with the likes of "Mr. Tambourine Man," "It's Alright Ma," "Gates of Eden," and "Desolation Row" has clearly met the challenge. But the point is that Dylan would never have created those masterpieces if he'd stayed constrained in the public's box. If he hadn't had the wherewithal to break out of the quicksand, he wouldn't have had the spark to invent new gems to supplement the older ones. You can appreciate Dylan's stunning body of work on one level, and that is fine. But if you truly want to understand his genius, you must recognize that it comes along with his lifelong quest to stay ahead of the baying pack and to think for himself. He will please himself, no matter what, even if it means throwing a curve ball now and then at the same people who have always loved his work. He just will not live on their terms.

Do you have the strength to shed the expectations of others? It isn't easy. Do you continually push yourself to change people's perceptions? Or are you content to show the same face, the same persona, the same output that you always have? If you admire Bob Dylan, you'll see that he has always been driven to be ambitious. That should be your mantra, too.

The China Syndrome

As you become more successful, you become a target. People begin to have expectations for you, and they expect nothing less than for you to live up to whatever they have in mind. When you don't, they can react in a fury because you have failed to live up to their ideal of you. You cannot, however, let them make you into a false symbol, regardless of the consequences of your actions and decisions. It's more important for you to remain true to yourself than to bend for someone else's whims. Once you've lost your principles, you've surrendered your integrity to the interests of the mob. And when that happens, then they do indeed own you, and you've lost everything.

Take, for instance, the occasion in early April 2011 when Dylan performed in China for the first time in his career. He withstood plenty of criticism because he wouldn't live up to everyone's ideal of him and didn't let other people push him around. In this episode, he illustrated the challenges you face when everyone wants a piece of you. When the word quickly spread that Dylan would play concerts in Beijing and Shanghai, people expected him to sing "The Times They Are a-Changin'" or another of his early social-protest gems to show his support for activists such as then-jailed artist Ai Weiwei, an outspoken critic of China's policies regarding democracy and human rights.

These are laudable causes, for sure, but Dylan, as always, resists being a pawn in other people's agenda. Since the early 1960s, advocates have demanded that Dylan be their leader. They expected him to be their spokesman, whether they were protesting the Vietnam War, nuclear power, apartheid, President Richard Nixon, or the wars in other places (El Salvador, Bosnia). Now as then, Dylan asserted his independence. He didn't sing "Blowin' in the Wind" or "The Times They Are a-Changin'" during his Beijing and Shanghai concerts and so braced himself for the backlash.

If you are going to assert your independence, you must inoculate yourself against critics. You must be prepared for people to second-guess your decisions and criticize you if you don't do as they think you should.

No less than Maureen Dowd in the *New York Times* blasted him in her April 10, 2011, column titled "Blowin' in the Idiot Wind," neatly combining two Dylan titles, "Blowin' in the Wind" and "Idiot Wind." Dowd began her commentary by saying, "Bob Dylan may have done the impossible; broken creative new ground in selling out."

Dowd personified the kinds of critics that he faced throughout his career. They failed to understand that Dylan was never going to be a poster boy for someone else's agenda.

Going Your Own Way

I wouldn't blame you if you rolled your eyes and said, "But Bob Dylan is a major star, so *of course* he can get away with making up or bending or ignoring the same rules I have to follow every day because I have a boss breathing down my neck twenty-four hours a day." What, then, if Dylan worked in an office, the kind where we toil away day after day in relative anonymity? Could he get away with the same sort of behavior and expect to ascend to the top of the organization chart? Sure, he could.

He showed the virtues of betting on himself on numerous occasions. True, Dylan is the ultimate example of someone who is gloriously self-employed, but don't let that fool you. Even Dylan has to answer to people in his life, such as the bean counters who run his record company, the concert promoters who book him in their halls, and especially you and me. Yes, we fans determine whether there will continue to be a market for Dylan's recordings and performances. He has to please us. But he does it, over and over, by showing us that he won't follow leaders—and he gives us hope because we can ignore leaders as well. Dylan, without even trying to, sets a worthy example for us to follow. And we, too, can do the same in our lives.

What it all comes down to is having an unshakable

faith in your ability to fend for yourself and a willingness to take charge of the decision-making process. In earlier chapters I talked about the necessity of finding your destiny, but this is something different.

The course of anyone's life can turn on a single decision because it can spark a series of changes. Taking charge is as much a state of mind as anything else. Once we have drilled into our heads the notion that we will be the master of our destiny, we are on our way to the thrilling feeling of self-discovery.

Nobody has to go rafting on a death-defying, grade-five river in Ecuador simply to prove his or her mettle. You can transform your life just fine by recognizing that you must make a change for any number of reasons, such as shaking out the cobwebs. Usually, however, we need to prove to ourselves—as well as to the other people in our sphere—that each of us is, indeed, our own boss.

Ten

BUILT TO LAST

In 2006, a television audience enjoyed a rare glimpse into the survival instinct of a uniquely American master. Spread over two parts and a few hours, Public Broadcasting System (PBS) stations informed and entertained viewers with a two-part documentary about Bob Dylan's life and music, titled *No Direction Home*. It spanned the period from his Minnesota roots to his English electric tour in 1966, when fans booed him at every stop. Think about that for a moment: These dedicated Dylan fans came to his shows and got so worked up that they took the rather extraordinary step of openly turning on their hero. That episode underscores why Dylan became a success in the first place and then continued to affect us decade after decade. He has a tremendous sense of self-reliance. He trusts no one other than himself. He believes he knows what to do to keep his audience surprised and entertained. He understands what it will take to remain in the game, while others who try to pander to the public's tastes invariably fail in their mission and slink out of view.

Above all, *No Direction Home* presented a portrait of Dylan as someone who had the fearlessness, perseverance, and restlessness required to make his mark and remain in our consciousness. Even though the documentary ends in 1966, a mere five years after Dylan burst on the popular culture scene in Greenwich Village as an unknown folksinger, nobody who watched the program would have been surprised to learn that he would go on and have a prominent musical career for many decades to come. Displaying a winner's swagger at all times, Dylan had what it took. Clearly, the man was intent on forging a legacy as a survivor—a lifer, not a flash in the pan—and he knew exactly how to attain that kind of rich success.

Can you say the same for yourself? Have you, as

Dylan has so famously done, guided yourself through your personal journey without a regard for what other people, however well meaning, advise you to do? I sure haven't. I wish I could tell you I showed supreme strength and resolve and told everyone else to take a hike. But I'd be lying—to you and to myself. I simply wasn't strong enough. Yes, I wish I had been, all along. I'm not ashamed, mind you. *Most* of us lack this will, don't we? It is probably a major factor in what separates the acknowledged geniuses from everyone else. Maybe Dylan wasn't the most talented musician in Greenwich Village back in the early 1960s, but he was likely the most ambitious. Sometimes, such as when he was accused of stealing his folksinger friends' songs and arrangements, Dylan could seem ruthless. So be it. He did have something going for him that others in the pack lacked: He had an unshakable faith in himself, which translated into an overwhelming sense of self-reliance. Call it an appreciation in his destiny, if you'd like. This enabled him to get out on a lonely stage in the first place, and return to it even when it seemed as though nothing were happening in his career and that audiences couldn't have cared less about him. That's how it was at the outset, but once Dylan found his creative voice, he was unstoppable.

Even as a youngster, Dylan was eager to challenge himself and make his dreams come true. Years before he had ever heard the music of Elvis Presley or Buddy Holly for the first time, Dylan had a clear vision of his destiny. He dreamed of someday enjoying a rich life as a working musician. Consider his telling recollection from a 1985 interview: "I always wanted to be a guitar player and a singer. Since I was ten, eleven or twelve, it was all that interested me. That was the only thing that I did that meant anything, really."

These three sentences are terribly instructive, as we trace Dylan's path to self-actualization. Dylan's path helps us understand that he was always extremely goal-oriented, right off the bat, and that his conviction to make it as a singer set him off on a path of thinking and acting in decisive and single-minded ways. At the outset, naturally, Dylan couldn't have even known what it took for a musician to get steady work, much less make it to the big time. Still, Dylan, it must be emphasized, never doubted his vision. He never equivocated in his pursuit of his goals. Nor did he fret about cobbling together a contingency plan. What for? There was never going to be a need for one, anyway.

The highly accomplished people among us, like Bob Dylan, invariably go through life with a laser focus. They don't sit still and wish for things to happen. They pursue their dream until it becomes an actuality. These folks are doers. They see life as a succession of interrelated objectives. They might regard each of their objectives the way that a motorist sees a series of markers on a highway. As they race past each one of them, they always insist on looking ahead. They see no reason to look back, so they don't bother.

But they do have a fixed destination. "I always wanted to be a guitar player and a singer," Dylan remembered. He put the pressure to achieve squarely on himself. He didn't lose any sleep about trying to impress his fans or satisfy the music critics or the sociologists or anybody else, for that matter. Bob Dylan had a lot to live up to in his own mind. And that makes all of the difference in our understanding about how he pursued success and achieved longevity. He did it by himself—for himself.

The *V* Word

Bob Dylan could never have risen to such dizzying heights as a musical and cultural icon, much less for fifty years, if he hadn't always possessed a sense of vision. Dylan is a genuine visionary. As a young man he saw something in himself and for himself that other people had never imagined could exist.

Ah, we now arrive at the all-important *V* word, one of the factors in life that can separate the winners from the dreamers. As we track his progress, we can define the term *vision* as always knowing where you want to go and recognizing how you intend to get there. As you go through the process of realizing your vision, you inevitably begin to recognize what is real and what is fake or artificial. "I don't really have a herd of astrologers telling me what's going to happen," Dylan told the interviewer and acclaimed novelist Jonathan Lethem in a *Rolling Stone* cover-story interview in 2006. "I just make one move after the other, this leads to that."

You could call Dylan the ultimate careerist—and it

would represent a ringing compliment to him. He has always kept his eyes on the prize. It follows that a central reason for his longevity is that he has disdained fads and trends. By their very nature, fads and trends exist in only the short term and don't have any lasting value. Dylan immediately knew that these never deserved a place in his life and work because they have no staying power. A careerist is all about having staying power. Dylan's musical brethren understand this point. "Once you've got it, you've got *it*," rock 'n' roll singer George Thorogood told me during a conversation in March 2011. "You go through periods and you got to stick it out. Any brilliant artist will stay brilliant—even if they aren't great in the commercial ways."

Dylan long understood that when you possess a strong vision for yourself, you get to make the rules. You live your life on your terms. You take the responsibility for making a decision and carrying it out. You decide what you must do. You act as your own boss. You gain an intuitive understanding of what is important. While other people tend to struggle about setting their priorities, you automatically know what matters, and you go after it. It can be daunting, scary even, to stand on your own. But the rewards are priceless.

Having a vision is another essential element in standing on your own two feet.

Don't be afraid to dream or even visualize your destiny. Dylan found inspiration, and perhaps comfort, in knowing that the world was tilted in his direction. We can understand this point from something he wrote in *Chronicles*, when he commented about his destiny at a point not long after he arrived in New York in 1961: "The whole city was dangling in front of my nose. I had a vivid idea of where everything was. The future was nothing to worry about. It was awfully close."

The (Bobby) Vee Factor

One of the most revealing—and poignant—moments in Dylan's entire half-century career occurred on a cold, late-autumn day in 1961, on a street in Brooklyn. Dressed in his scruffy folksinger rags, Dylan had ridden the D train from Greenwich Village down to the Paramount Theater on Flatbush Avenue so he could renew a friendship with Bobby Vee. Everything about Vee, starting with his teen-idol made-up name to his silk suits, narrow tie, and perfect brown hair, screamed pop star, whereas Dylan was the epitome of the Village folkie.

In the summer of 1960, Dylan auditioned for Vee's band in Fargo, North Dakota, not far from Dylan's native Hibbing, as a piano player. But Vee didn't need one, and Dylan took the hint. The rebuke may have disappointed him because he then saw Vee as something of a kindred spirit. "We had the same musical history and came from the same place at the same time," Dylan wrote affectionately in *Chronicles*. Why did Dylan go and visit Vee at that time, late in 1961? Perhaps it was important to Dylan for Vee, a major star on the Los Angeles pop-music scene, to know that Dylan was starting to make progress himself in gritty New York City.

Dylan seemed to feel a sense of satisfaction, as he wrote in his book: "I told him I was playing in the folk clubs, but it was impossible to give him any indication of what it was all about. His only reference would have been the Kingston Trio, Brothers Four, stuff like that. He'd become a crowd pleaser in the pop world."

At the time of their meeting, Vee was one of the most successful singers in the teenybopper market. Dylan, of course, was anything but. After all, aspiring teen idols didn't take the name of a Welsh poet who drank too much and died an unceremonious death. We can't get inside Dylan's head and guess whether he was envious or even impressed by Vee's success as a chart-topping pop singer of fluffy confectionary tunes. We can assume, however, that Dylan was not. He wanted something bigger, deeper, and more meaningful from his life's calling than recording a string of mindless hits. Even then, Dylan had the point of view of a careerist, someone who had a long view about his chosen profession. Instead of instant fame, he unabashedly pursued longevity. Indeed, within a few months of his meeting with Bobby Vee, Dylan would write "Blowin' in the Wind," one of the most iconic songs in popular music history. He couldn't have created it if he had been intent on pursuing pop stardom. By instructive contrast, Dylan took pride in looking as scruffy as possible. He sang about nobody's angst but his own. It was inconceivable that Dylan would sing "Suzie Baby" or any of Vee's other hits in his Greenwich Village folk haunts.

Vee helped remind Dylan about the true meaning of success and the price you have to pay to attain it. Dylan understood intuitively that his old friend had become nothing more than the latest confection in a music industry that eagerly chewed up the likes of Bobby Vee and Bobby Rydell and Bobby Vinton as well as so many others—and then cruelly spat them out. They were lucky, this brigade of Bobbys, if their careers lasted as long as the shine in their stage suits.

Dylan lets us know that he drew a line between the likes of Vee and himself. "He'd become a crowd pleaser in the pop world," Dylan wrote of Vee in his memoir. It's easy to figure out that Dylan didn't see that kind of life for himself. You could count on one hand the number of times Dylan set out to please a crowd on its own terms. "As for myself, I had nothing against pop songs, but the definition of pop was changing. They just didn't seem to be as good as they ever were." We see, time and again, that Dylan refused to compromise his values. He walked off *The Ed Sullivan Show*, and he moved on from pleasing the crowd who demanded that he rewrite "Blowin' in the Wind" again and again. His encounter with Bobby Vee was as dramatic as any moment. Here, he came face to face with a false destiny, and he walked away from it.

It takes inner strength to remain true to yourself when you can see a peer getting ahead by following another path. It requires you to remember what you care about, what kind of aura you want to project. We have all known somebody like Bobby Vee in our own lives. Not that Vee represented anything sordid or inherently evil, mind you. But we can discern that he was not built to last, that he was perfectly content to be a short-timer, that he couldn't or wouldn't push himself to challenge the manufactured image that other people had created for him. Vee would never have what it takes to thrive in his field over a long period of time. Vee and others like him allow themselves to be manipulated. There are people like Bobby Vee working happily in every office in America, yours and mine included.

How Do You See Yourself?

Look around at any highly accomplished individuals. It could be business leaders like Steve Jobs or Secretary of State Hillary Clinton or director Steven Spielberg or even the innovative basketball guru Phil Jackson. It could well be you, too. Like Dylan, they approach the world with a resounding sense of purpose and an ability to solve problems that threaten to throw them off course.

We can also see how this early musical ambition lit the fire for Dylan's remarkably durable career, occurring in an industry in which a one-hit wonder is the rule and not the exception. This also serves as our starting point to assess how Dylan eventually grew up to become such an inspiration and a role model for so many people around the world. By contrast, most young boys fantasize about fighting fires or playing Major League Baseball. Bob Dylan, however, had distinct, well-thought-out ideas all his own. The difference is that most kids grow out of those ideas and become something else. Perhaps they decided to do something more conventional, if not achievable, and studied to become accountants or teachers or doctors.

By Dylan's own account, he had already sealed his destiny by the age of ten. What makes this revelation all the more astonishing is how unlikely it must have seemed for a lad from the Iron Range of Hibbing, Minnesota, to harbor such grand hopes at such an embryonic point. Nor did Dylan have any kind of track record of success. Far from being recognized in his small town as a prodigy, he was all but hooted off the stage at Hibbing High School for his wild, loud rock 'n' roll stylings during a talent contest. Yet he never wavered.

And what about you? How serious are you about pursuing your goal? Even if you didn't know what you wanted to be when you grew up, do you now possess Dylan's uncommon measure of commitment?

Steering with Your Personal Compass

Dylan had a laser focus about his future probably since he heard the first record that ever affected him, "Drifting Too Far from the Shore," by Bill Monroe and the Bluegrass Boys. As he described the experience in the Martin Scorsese documentary *No Direction Home*, it is clear that Dylan was never tortured by indecision. He wasn't dogged by self-doubt. Nor was he limited in the scope of his ambition. Because he had a rock-solid sense of self, he could see the finish line even before the race got under way.

Vision. Commitment. Determination. Action. These were Bob Dylan's building blocks to success, and they marked his progress at each crucial juncture, dating from his upbringing in Hibbing to his college time in Minneapolis to his sink-or-swim indoctrination in Greenwich Village. We all have a destiny.

We all can't know at the age of ten what we want to do with the rest of our lives. It may be a blessing (or even a curse) to have such a conviction at an impossibly young and unformed time in our lives. But we've all felt that kind of inner drive at some point. The question is, has it propelled us forward, or did we let it languish?

Dylan didn't arrive in Greenwich Village as an acknowledged star. He gladly paid his dues, proved to be a voracious learner, and remained ambitious at every turn. But even when others didn't see him as a winner, he did.

We can all learn from that kid, though, barely out of elementary school, who knew what he wanted. He already had a goal in mind. He had an absolute conviction about what he wanted to do with the rest of his life. Crucially, this dreamer had the determination to make his dreams come true.

There is another component to this jigsaw puzzle that we call our life, and it is a very big piece. This involves having a personal code of behavior, which will guide you throughout your journey from here to there. It means everything, because this will determine what you will do, and won't do, to get to the finish line.

Dylan has always had a solid compass. It has been his secret weapon, keeping him forever grounded and focused. We wonder, how did Dylan rise to such dizzying heights to thrive in the cutthroat entertainment industry for five decades? I point you to Dylan's code as a major reason for his remarkable longevity.

He never became overwhelmed by fads or trends in the music world. Clearly, he has had the capacity to understand that his journey is a marathon, not a sprint, and that he would encounter numerous temptations along the way that could potentially distract or even destroy him.

When Dylan's fans contemplate his legacy, it's easy to focus on his songwriting brilliance or his insistence on remaining enigmatic as a method to keep just out of reach of his critics. We can recall the many historic concerts he has given and participated in, but it is instructive to remember that Dylan started out his life's work as a ten-year-old boy who set out to be a guitar player and a singer.

Bob Dylan hailed from Hibbing, Minnesota, a remote area located in the northwest part of the state, which was so desolate that the natives had dubbed it the Iron Range. Considering his hometown, you could say that all Dylan had when he was growing up there were his dreams. Of course, every success story has always started with someone's dream. And the odds always seem long indeed.

Dylan has been a fixture in our lives, one way or another, for so long that we sometimes take him for granted. We can look at his remarkable longevity as an influential guitar player and singer, and we will assume that success for this gifted man must have always been a given. But the truth was far from that. If you think Dylan was preordained for success, guess again. Adding to the improbable nature of his triumphs, we can understand that the odds were stacked heavily against him from the very start. This shows us that it doesn't matter where, or how, we start out in our lives. What makes all of the difference is what we do with what we have at our disposal.

Like a Rolling Stone

It's hardly revolutionary for me to suggest that Dylan's song "Like a Rolling Stone," recorded at the first session he ever conducted with the idea of making a hit single, marked a turning point in his career and truly made official his journey from folk to rock 'n' roll music. Journalists and Dylan buffs have discussed this fine point for decades. Yes, it is infectious, with its strains of a "La Bamba" beat, but the most intriguing aspect of "Like a Rolling Stone" goes well beyond the unforgettable, snarling vocal or the powerful musical accompaniment. People will invariably point to such strengths as Dylan's joyous, in-your-face vocal; the catchy, oft-repeated "How-does-it-feel?" chorus; and Al Kooper's pulsating organ riffs. All of these qualities are worthy of kudos, but there is something else that underscores Dylan's all-in watchword much more effectively.

We frequently seem to overlook another dynamic that helps the song stand out: the sheer length of the song, which underscores how radical it really was for those times. Clocking in at about six minutes, "Like a Rolling Stone" was, up to that point, easily the longest 45 rpm record ever released. As inventive as the Beatles were or as antiestablishment as the Rolling Stones had a reputation for being, neither of those two English bands had ever dreamed of putting out a six-minute-long song for AM radio airplay. It was just not done, because the music establishment had ordained that a single should last between two and three minutes—and that was it. This kind of a song was easy to market to youngsters, who had short attention spans anyway. For that matter, Columbia Records surely had its doubts, too, as to whether disc jockeys would embrace a song of that length. After all, the Beatles, who ruled AM radio at the time, had in 1965 audaciously released "Ticket to Ride," their first hit single that actually exceeded the vaunted barrier of *three* minutes. And even that seemed like a milestone of sorts at the time.

If he had listened to the ever-present suits in his life, he would surely have cut off "Like a Rolling Stone" at the three-minute mark and let the song blend in with all of the other offerings that people heard on the radio in the summer of 1965. How boring that had been for him, though! The song would have never had such a special place in Dylan's catalog. As usual, he was way ahead of everyone else, and as usual, he broke new ground.

Dylan is showing us the importance of creating a legacy for ourselves, on our own terms. Dylan has long exemplified the inherent wisdom of trusting your gut and making your own decisions, of thinking for yourself. As Greil Marcus, the author of the informative and thought-provoking 2005 book *Like a Rolling Stone*, pointed out: "To Dylan, 'Like a Rolling Stone' was a single the minute he walked out of the studio, if not the minute he walked into it." This single-mindedness, characteristic of Dylan at his best and most inventive, enabled him to have the vision and the conviction to do what had never been done before.

The living, breathing history of this great song lives on. Sure, it succeeded on its merits, but it remains today Dylan's most requested number in concert. He usually closes his shows around the world with "Like a Rolling Stone" or plays it in the dramatic next-to-last slot. Dylan clearly cherishes the tune as much as the people in the audience do.

Tomorrow Is Today

Do you reach for the stars and kiss the sky? I suspect that for most of us, the answer is no. Why not? There's no disgrace in being less than what we are capable of achieving, but what it boils down to is that most of us aren't willing to commit to what we need to do to achieve our highest goals. We rationalize our lot in life by secretly assuring ourselves that it all didn't really matter so much anyway.

Dylan tells us differently. He made specific decisions that enabled him to have such accomplishments as Grammy awards, an Oscar, number one albums, and sold-out concerts around the world, not to mention a legacy as one of the most innovative and original artists of our time.

What can we glean from Dylan's experience? First, reinvention means everything: Dylan innately recognized that he couldn't go on by simply reaching the same audience as the same old Dylan. He wasn't a can of Coca-Cola, in which the public wanted the same piece of merchandise every time. In the 1960s, his particular genius—besides his songwriting and singing, of course— was to shift from one style to another, going from Woody Guthrie–like talking-blues numbers to protest songs to introspective lyrics to rock 'n' roll to country pie. He constantly confounded the fans and the critics, who found it nearly impossible to pin him down.

He performed the same trick on his Never Ending Tour. He went in front of audiences a hundred times a year, beginning in 1988, but they never knew what they were going to get. One outcome was certain: When they left the theater, they had seen a viable legend, not just a museum piece.

When Success Is the Enemy of Future Success

Dylan also teaches us to never rest on our laurels. It is tempting, though, to coast through life once we have achieved some success. Not Dylan. He knows current success is the enemy of future success, and so should you.

One thing about Dylan, he always keeps us guessing. When Dylan appeared on MTV's *Unplugged* in November 1994, he played a rather rocking set of old material. His effort was rewarded, as the subsequent album from the sets reached twenty-three on the U.S. charts and number ten in the United Kingdom. It seemed likely to assume, then, that he would follow this pattern on his next album. Wrong again. Dylan was up to his old tricks by going in the opposite direction. He was back in charge of his career, and he was going to do it his own way.

Even though Dylan has seemingly been around forever, he is also forever in the stage of starting out— because every new stage of his life is in its own way a test of his vitality in the marketplace. Maybe Dylan understands that this is how it really is in our world: You and only you are responsible for your destiny.

Conclusion

UP TO ME

We can glean a great deal about Dylan's thought process by examining a statement he made in 1985, when he was discussing the turning points of his career to that moment. It was revealing to note what Dylan said when he compared two points in his life: when he was booed by audiences during his early electric concerts in 1965 and 1966, and when he was cheered by legions of fans across North America on his triumphant 1974 comeback tour. He told Cameron Crowe: "Time had proven them all wrong." This is a revealing statement, underscoring Dylan's mind-set.

One of Bob Dylan's everlasting lessons has always been this point: Don't ever feel compelled to substitute flash for substance. In our celebrity culture, this is easy to do; but what happens when, sooner or later, the flash becomes a flash in the pan? It doesn't matter, either, what your status is at a given moment, whether you happen to be standing at the beginning or closer to the end of your journey. Having enough faith in yourself is what really matters now and forever. Understand what you bring to the equation and stand by it. Realize you possess the inner power, wits, drive, and self-awareness to make it possible for you to get where you want to go.

Dylan practices what he preaches. It's easier said than done, especially in the midst of a blinding media glare. Remarkably, he seems to have found a way to live his life with the same values both before fame came to him and after he became universally recognized. When I read his book *Chronicles*, which traces his early days in New York City up to his period of stardom, I noticed that the writer's attitude doesn't really change too much throughout the volume. Whether Dylan is writing about his raga-muffin origins in Greenwich Village, when he frequently crashed at friends' apartments, or the "Oh Mercy" block, when he is struggling to find a new musical approach at a time when he was an acknowledged superstar, the author's point of view about himself remains consistent. He is unpretentious at all times. It is an admirable trait.

Fans and pundits point all the time to the many musical changes that Dylan has experienced. But these are all on the surface. Regardless of what Dylan is singing about, or how he is doing it, he is carrying on with a personal code that we can learn from. He demonstrates the importance of remaining single-minded even in the face of adversity; of never giving into the whims of critics or the temptations of fads; and of summoning the strength time and again to feel comfortable as the eternal outsider, to remain self-confident and focused in good and bad times alike, and, above all, to stay true to yourself.

During his five decades in the public eye, Bob Dylan has received accolades ranging from spokesman to genius. He has been lauded for his music, his artistic vision, and his humanity. He deserves all of these rich designations.

But let's remember to include one more apt term to describe this unique man, Bob Dylan: role model.

Acknowledgments

"People need to be encouraged, not stepped on and put in a straight jacket," Bob Dylan mused to interviewer Cameron Crowe in 1985.

Dylan knows his stuff. An author cherishes encouragement, and I was lucky in this respect. Plenty of kind people offered their advice, good wishes, and expertise.

My parents, Pat and Phil Friedman, are my biggest fans, and they mean everything to me. Much love to my wonderful sister, Carla, and her husband, Rob Karen, and to my all-knowing brother, Larry (who got me started on this path when he convinced me to spend my allowance on my first album, *Meet the Beatles!*), and his wife, Leslie.

I could never have written this book without my agent and friend, Lynn Johnston, the best cheerleader/drill sergeant I know. A big thank-you to Maria Gagliano, my trusty editor. Thanks as well to John Duff and the rest of the team at Perigee.

Every journalist should have a great boss like David Callaway, the editor in chief of MarketWatch. I also owe a big debt to my commentary teammates Angela Moore, David Weidner, and Therese Poletti.

People from the music world were generous and instructive, including Robbie Robertson, Jonathan Taplin, Arthur Rosato, Ronee Blakley, Suzanne Vega, Harvey Brooks, Chris Difford, George Thorogood, Nick Mason, Tom Cording, Carol Fenelon, Ken Regan, Russ Titleman, Joel Bernstein, Bob Merlis, Dennis McNally, David Gans, and Steve Berkowitz. Even a two-minute conversation with Paul Simon (during a rain delay at Yankee Stadium, no less!) offered insight into how much musicians respect Dylan. And I want to thank very much those of you who helped but didn't want to see your names in print.

A shout-out to some special people: Danny Small,

ACKNOWLEDGMENTS

Stuart Cohn, Andy Axler, Philip Dinhofer, Michael
Dinhofer, Dana Gordon, Kathy Burton, Hui-yong Yu,
Nell Minow, Anthony de Curtis, Jen Naidich, Christo-
pher Ruddy, Harold Derschowitz, Anne Margaret Dan-
iel, Paul Bizzigotti, Charles Davlin, Angela Kohler,
Philip Bashe, Thomas Kostigen, Vernon Silver, Matt
Rees, Scott Soshnick, Anthony Mason, Peter Feld, Phil
Panasci, Jeff Slate, Bob Levinson, Tom Noonan, Frank
Beacham, Bob Brown, George Lois, Keith Kelly, Steven
Levy, Emily Church, Steve "the Dude" Gelsi, Brian
Bremner, Jeff Rothfeder, Shasta, Jim Fusilli, John Jur-
gensen, Christopher John Farley, Alexandra Cheney,
Barbara Chai, Amy Dockser Marcus, Brian Steinberg,
Steven Kotok, Jessica Tartell, Liz Alderman, Keith Rich-
burg, Tish Cohen, Norman Ratner, Geoff Boucher, John
Fugelsang, Sharon Hyman, David Evans, Robert Daniel,
Michael Burns, Linda Beltz Glaser, Judith Beltz, Harold
Lepidus, Karl Erik Anderson, Julie Spira, Sheila Weller,
Sarah Needleman, and Jamie Stiehm. Thank you to Meg
Hirshberg, Erin Arvedlund, and Suzanne Woolley, who
read early chapters. Annie Davlin inspired me until the
un-bitter end.

222

Dylan Nation is vast and global. Thanks to the wondrous Mitch Blank, ExpectingRain.com, the Bob Dylan Examiner, EDLIS, and other websites. These authors helped shape my thinking: Bob Dylan, Greil Marcus, Toby Thompson, Robert Shelton, Jon Landau, Anthony Scaduto, Larry "Ratso" Sloman, Clinton Heylin, Tim Riley, Sean Wilentz, Robert Hilburn, Bill Flanagan, Howard Sounes, Jonathan Cott, Michael Gray, Ben Fong-Torres, and John Bauldie. So did Jann Wenner, Matt Damsker, Mary Travers, Dave Herman, editors at *Rolling Stone* and *Mojo*, Douglas Brinkley, Jonathan Lethem, Ron Rosenbaum, Kurt Loder, Al Aronowitz, Nat Hentoff, Neil Hickey, Mikal Gilmore, and others who interviewed Dylan.

Bob Dylan once said of his hero Woody Guthrie: "He had so much to give! You could listen to his songs and actually learn how to live."

Well, Bob, that's pretty much how I and so many other people feel about you.

Every Grain of Dylan

SOME OF THE BEST OF THE BEST
DYLAN CHRONICLERS

Dylan is said to be press-shy, but the truth is that he has probably conducted more interviews than any other musician in his fifty years as a recording artist.

Unfortunately, Dylan can choose to be famously oblique when he talks with journalists, although he has also come across brilliantly on a number of occasions. These are my seven favorite interviews:

- In 1964, music writer Nat Hentoff captured the essence of the young folkie Dylan in a profile for the *New Yorker*. Hentoff wrote about Dylan as he was recording the final of his four early folk albums, *Another Side of Bob Dylan*, during the early 1960s. There is no hint here that Dylan would turn to rock 'n' roll the following year.

- When Dylan returned to the road in early 1974, he was a hot story, and it's a good bet that every major media outlet in America tried to corner him for an exclusive. In a beautifully written piece, Ben Fong-Torres of *Rolling Stone* followed Dylan around early in the tour and found him in a rare reflective mood.

- Things were different some twenty-one months later, in very late 1975. Dylan had again gone on tour, but this was the ramshackle Rolling Thunder Revue. Journalist Larry "Ratso" Sloman carried on a rollicking, extended dialogue with Dylan in New York City, New England, and parts of Canada. Sloman succeeded where so many interviewers had failed by winning his trust and earning his friendship. Sloman managed to find Dylan utterly relaxed throughout their sessions, and Dylan rewarded the man they lovingly called Ratso with the most sweeping set of interviews he had ever granted.

• I have a sneaky fondness for Neil Hickey's interview with Dylan, published in *TV Guide* during the summer of 1976. The two of them drove around greater Los Angeles on the eve of the broadcast of *Hard Rain*, a one-hour documentary of Dylan's concert in Fort Collins, Colorado, during the tail end of the second leg of the Rolling Thunder Revue. Dylan was positively chatty, saying at one point, memorably, that America should have built statues for the Beatles.

• Dylan was his most candid of any interview when he spoke with *Philadelphia Evening Bulletin* writer Matt Damsker on the afternoon of September 15, 1978, in Augusta, Maine. The occasion was especially interesting, as their conversation took place only several hours before the first concert of his 1978 U.S. tour. Dylan is very much at ease with Damsker, and even talks about his family, which he seldom does. Dylan doesn't back away from any of Damsker's probing questions.

- Dylan spoke eloquently and with great conviction when he talked with journalist and filmmaker Cameron Crowe for the expansive liner notes of his retrospective album *Biograph* in 1985. Dylan goes over his entire life during this wide-ranging dialogue. He provides more information about himself here than in any other interview. Until Dylan published his memoir in 2004, this booklet was the best source if someone wanted to know what Dylan was thinking.

- In 2009, Dylan was on tour in Europe when he consented to an interview with historian Douglas Brinkley for *Rolling Stone*. It was around the time that Dylan's studio album *Together Through Life* was being released worldwide. Of all the pieces I've read on Dylan, this is my all-time favorite. Brinkley shrewdly prompted Dylan to give his thoughts on a number of subjects, ranging from the circumstances surrounding his walking off *The Ed Sullivan Show* in 1963 to his deep appreciation of his native Minnesota.

Resources

Barnes, Barry, *Everything I Know About Business I Learned from the Grateful Dead*, Business Press, 2011.

Bauldie, John (editor), *Wanted Man*, Citadel Press, 1990.

Boyd, Pattie, *Wonderful Tonight*, Harmony Books, 2007.

Clapton, Eric, *Clapton*, Broadway Books, 2007.

Collins, Judy, *Sweet Judy Blue Eyes*, Crown Archetype, 2011.

Cott, Jonathan (editor), *Bob Dylan: The Essential Interviews*, Wenner Books, 2006.

DeCurtis, Anthony, *In Their Words*, Hal Leonard Corp., 2005.

Dylan, Bob, *Chronicles: Volume One*, Simon & Schuster, 2004.

Eisen, Jonathan (editor), *The Age of Rock*, Random House, 1969.

Ellison, James, *Younger Than That Now*, Thunder's Mouth Press, 2004.

Epstein, Daniel Mark, *The Ballad of Bob Dylan*, HarperCollins, 2011.

Flanagan, Bill, *Written in My Soul*, Contemporary Books, 1986.

Fong-Torres, Ben (editor), *Knockin' on Dylan's Door*, Straight Arrow Publishers, 1974.

Gill, Andy, and Kevin Odegard, *A Simple Twist of Fate*, Da Capo, 2004.

Goodman, Fred, *The Mansion on the Hill*, Times Books, 1997.

Gray, Michael, *The Bob Dylan Encyclopedia*, Continuum International, 2006.

Griffin, Sid, *Million Dollar Bash*, Jawbone Press, 2007.

Hadju, David, *Positively 4th Street*, Farrar, Straus and Giroux, 2001.

Heylin, Clinton, *Behind the Shades*, William Morrow, 2001.

———, *Revolution in the Air*, Chicago Review Press, 2009.

———, *Still on the Road*, Chicago Review Press, 2010.

Hilburn, Robert, *Cornflakes with John Lennon*, Rodale, 2009.

Isaacson, Walter, *Steve Jobs*, Simon & Schuster, 2011.

Landau, Jon, *It's Too Late to Stop Now*, Straight Arrow Books, 1972.

Lee, C. P., *Like the Night*, Helter Skelter Publishing, 1998.

Marcus, Greil, *Bob Dylan: Writings 1968–2010*, Public Affairs, 2011.

———, *Like a Rolling Stone*, Public Affairs, 2005.

———, *Mystery Train*, E. P. Dutton, 1975.

Marsh, Dave, *The Beatles Second Album*, Rodale, 2007.

McGregor, Craig (editor), *Bob Dylan: A Retrospective*, William Morrow, 1972.

O'Dell, Chris, *Miss O'Dell*, Touchstone, 2009.

Richards, Keith, *Life*, Little, Brown, 2010.

Riley, Tim, *Hard Rain*, Alfred A. Knopf, 1992.

———, *Lennon*, Hyperion, 2011.

Rotolo, Suze, *A Freewheelin' Time*, Random House, 2008.

Santelli, Robert, *The Bob Dylan Scrapbook, 1956–1966*, Simon & Schuster, 2005.

Scaduto, Anthony, *Dylan*, Signet, 1971.

Sheff, David, *The Playboy Interviews with John Lennon and Yoko Ono*, Playboy Press, 1981.

Shelton, Robert, *No Direction Home*, Da Capo, 1986.

Shepard, Sam, *The Rolling Thunder Logbook*, Da Capo, 2004.

Sloman, Larry, *On the Road with Bob Dylan*, Three Rivers Press, 1978.

Smith, Patti, *Just Kids*, Ecco, 2010.

Sounes, Howard, *Down the Highway*, Grove Press, 2001.

Taplin, Jonathan, *Outlaw Blues*, Annenberg Press, 2011.

Thompson, Toby, *Positively Main Street*, University of Minnesota, 2008.

Weiner, Howard F., *Tangled Up in Tunes*, Pencil Hill Publishing, 2012.

Wenner, Jann S., *Lennon Remembers*, Straight Arrow Publishers, 1971.

Wenner, Jann S., and Joe Levy, *The Rolling Stone Interviews*, Back Bay Books, 2007.

Wilentz, Sean, *Bob Dylan in America*, Doubleday, 2010.

Willliams, Paul, *Bob Dylan: Performing Artist 1960–1973*, Underwood-Miller, 1990.

———, *Bob Dylan: Performing Artist 1974–1986*, Omnibus Press, 2004.

———, *Bob Dylan: Performing Artist 1986–1990 & Beyond*, Omnibus Press, 2005.

———, *Dylan: What Happened?*, Entwhistle Books, 1979.

———, *Watching the River Flow*, Omnibus Press, 1996

About the Author

Photo by Amanda Gordon

Jon Friedman writes the Media Web column for MarketWatch .com. He also covered Wall Street for Bloomberg News, *USA Today*, *BusinessWeek*, and *Investor's Business Daily*. He is the coauthor of *House of Cards: Inside the Troubled Empire of American Express*. Friedman, who lives and works in New York City, saw his first Bob Dylan concert in 1974 and has maintained a lifetime appreciation of Dylan's music and legacy.